Bomber Command Airfields of Yorkshire

Bomber Command Airfields of Yorkshire

Peter Jacobs

Pen & Sword
AVIATION

First published in Great Britain in 2017 by
Pen & Sword Aviation
An imprint of Pen & Sword Books Ltd
47 Church Street
Barnsley
South Yorkshire
S70 2AS

ISBN 978 1 78346 331 2

A CIP catalogue record for this book is available from the British Library

Typeset in 10pt Palatino by Mac Style, Driffield, East Yorkshire
Printed and bound in the UK by CPI Group (UK) Ltd, Croydon, CRO 4YY

Pen & Sword Books Ltd incorporates the Imprints of Pen & Sword Aviation, Pen & Sword Maritime, Pen & Sword Military, Wharncliffe Local History, Pen & Sword Select, Pen & Sword Military Classics, Leo Cooper, Remember When, Seaforth Publishing and Frontline Publishing

For a complete list of Pen & Sword titles please contact
PEN & SWORD BOOKS LIMITED
47 Church Street, Barnsley, South Yorkshire, S70 2AS, England
E-mail: enquiries@pen-and-sword.co.uk
Website: www.pen-and-sword.co.uk

Contents

Acknowledgements

This is my fifth book on RAF airfields during the Second World War as part of the *Aviation Heritage Trail* series, and the second relating to Bomber Command following *Bomber Command Airfields of Lincolnshire*. Many people have helped me along the way, in particular I would like to thank: Ian Ross, the Chief Engineer at the Royal Aeroplane Club (Breighton); Matthew Ellis, Ian Myles and John Stirk at the Burn Gliding Club (Burn); Liz Bamford at the RAF College Cranwell; the Circuit Manager at the Croft Circuit (Croft); Ian Reed (Museum Director) and Ian Richardson (Communications Manager) at the Yorkshire Air Museum (Elvington); Simon Pocklington (the owner), Cas Smith (Chief Flying Instructor) and Carrie at the Full Sutton Flying Centre (Full Sutton); Group Captain David Bradshaw (Station Commander), Squadron Leader Alfie Hall (Historical Training Facility) and Lynn Dunne (Media Communications Officer) at RAF Leeming; Group Captain Iain Lang (Station Commander), Wing Commander (Ret'd) Alan Mawby (Curator of the Memorial Room), Dick Arthurs (Assistant Curator) and Flight Lieutenant Mike Lumsden (Media Communications Officer) at RAF Linton-on-Ouse; Kevin Bryett (Chairman, 158 Squadron Association), Alison Mottershead (Secretary, 158 Squadron Association) and Peter Naylor (Lissett); Tonita Day at the Wolds Gliding Club (Pocklington); Alan Swales and Pat at the York Gliding Centre (Rufforth); and Jacqui Watts (Snaith).

I must also thank Seb Cox and his staff at the Air Historical Branch (RAF) at RAF Northolt for their help over so many years. As far as other sources of information are concerned, I would like to pay tribute to Martin Middlebrook and Chris Everitt for their excellent book *The Bomber Command War Diaries: An*

Operational Reference Book 1939–1945. I have always considered this book to be the authoritative work when it comes to facts and figures about Bomber Command during the Second World War. When it comes to squadrons and aircraft types I always use James J Halley's excellent book *Squadrons of the Royal Air Force and Commonwealth 1918–1988*, which I consider to be the best and most consistent record under one cover. As for the illustrations in this book, many have been generously provided by individuals over the years or have come from the AHB or Imperial War Museum, and so I thank everyone who has helped me with images over the years, in particular my former RAF colleague Ken Delve.

It only leaves me to say thank you to all those who served with Bomber Command during the Second World War. Without their remarkable contribution there would be no stories to be told. I must also thank the management and staff at Pen and Sword, in particular Laura Hirst for all her effort behind the scenes to turn my work into the publication you see today.

Introduction

During nearly six years of the Second World War only one force on the Allied side was continuously involved in active operations against Nazi Germany – RAF Bomber Command. Bomber Command had entered the war with fifty-five squadrons spread across five operational groups, with the Yorkshire-based 4 Group, headquartered at Linton-on-Ouse, equipped with the twin-engine Armstrong Whitworth Whitley medium bomber; eight squadrons were based at four of the county's airfields with a further two squadrons of Handley Page Hampdens belonging to 5 Group based in South Yorkshire.

A series of pre-war expansion schemes would see an increase in the number of bomber airfields in eastern England, including Yorkshire, but it would take time for these to be complete with the last not ready until 1943. They were, however, all based on a standard bomber airfield design with three concrete/tarmac hardened runways, all connected by a perimeter track off which hard standings were constructed for the dispersal of aircraft. The airfields included various hangars and other technical, administrative and domestic buildings, depending on where and when they were constructed, with station personnel accommodated in a variety of ways; ranging from being housed in the local community to purpose-built brick buildings on base to temporary Nissen huts that proved to be cold and draughty in winter.

Along with 5 Group's Hampdens and the Vickers Wellingtons of 3 Group, Yorkshire's Whitley squadrons bore the brunt of Bomber Command's early campaign. Indeed, Whitleys were involved in Bomber Command's first operations of the war when ten aircraft dropped propaganda leaflets over Germany; an operation known as *Nickelling*.

Bomber Command's operational airfields in Yorkshire and County Durham during the Second World War. Non-operational airfields are not shown, they are: Acaster Malbis (south of York); Cottam (south of Driffield); Marston Moor (north-west of Rufforth); Plainville (north of York); Riccall (north-west of Breighton); and Wombleton (north-east of East Moor). The emergency landing ground at Carnaby is north of Lissett. Doncaster and Lindholme are near their main airfield of Finningley in South Yorkshire, none of which were part of 4 Group or 6 (RCAF) Group, while the factory airfield of Yeadon is to the north-west of Leeds in West Yorkshire and off the map. (Author)

The dropping of leaflets was hardly offensive and it would be a long time before bombs were dropped on German soil, and so for now propaganda leaflets were all the crews of Bomber Command were allowed to drop. During the first month of the war more than 20 million leaflets were dropped. For Britain, those early days of the Second World War were more about caution than aggression with the leaflets carrying a *'warning message from Great Britain'*, informing those who read them that the war had been brought about by the policies of the Nazis and was not in the interest of the German people.

Much of the period of the so-called Phoney War was spent in this way or laying mines, or perhaps carrying out reconnaissance sorties or anti-shipping attacks, but at that stage of the war the bombing of mainland Germany remained forbidden. It would take a German raid against the Royal Navy at Scapa Flow in March 1940, a raid where bombs were dropped on land and resulted in the death of one civilian with several more wounded, for Bomber Command to be ordered to carry out a reprisal raid against a German seaplane base on the southernmost tip of the island of Sylt in northern Germany. The attack involved Yorkshire's Whitleys and was Bomber Command's first real bombing raid of the war, but despite crews claiming success the post-raid reconnaissance revealed no damage and merely reinforced the difficulty of operating at night.

With the exception of the Wellington, perhaps, the RAF's early medium bombers of the Second World War had been found lacking in modern air warfare. In simple terms, Bomber Command was not equipped for the role that it had been assigned. It was not large enough to operate as a strategic independent bombing force, its technological capability was lacking and bombing methods still lacked accuracy.

Germany's invasion of France and the Low Countries in May 1940 brought a long overdue change in bombing strategy. Finally, bomber crews were permitted to attack targets east of the Rhine, including the industrial heartland of Germany, the Ruhr. Gradually, Bomber Command's raids began to increase in size but there was still no concentration of effort against a single target. However, that changed on the night of 23/24 September 1940 when Bomber Command sent 129 aircraft, including Yorkshire's Whitleys, to Berlin with some success.

For Bomber Command, the first year of war had achieved little in the way of bombing success, other than to show that Britain was far from defeated and was capable of hitting back. But things were about to change. In February 1941 the first of the RAF's new and heavier bombers, the Short Stirling, entered service. This was soon followed by the second, the Avro Manchester, and then the third, the Handley Page Halifax, made its operational debut.

Yorkshire was to be home to the Halifax for the rest of the war. It was a vast improvement over the Whitley that it would eventually replace, making 4 Group an all-Halifax group. Bomber Command could now spread its effort far and wide but by the end of the year it could still only muster fifty-six squadrons, of which only one-quarter consisted of the newer and heavier bombers. Additionally, there were still problems as far as bombing accuracy was concerned; only one bomb in ten was estimated to be falling within five miles of its intended target.

The RAF still lacked enough heavy bombers and the capability to win a decisive strategic bombing campaign, but 1942 proved to be a crucial year for Bomber Command and marked a turning point in its fortunes. First, after frequent changes of commander,

A Whitley crew pictured early in the war. The Whitley was at the heart of the Yorkshire-based 4 Group's effort during the opening exchanges of hostilities. (via Ken Delve)

Following several changes at the head of Bomber Command, Air Marshal Arthur Harris was appointed at its head in February 1942. Harris would inspire and lead the command for the rest of the war. (AHB)

it appointed at its head the man who was to inspire and lead it for the rest of the war, Air Marshal Arthur Harris, and then the Avro Lancaster entered operational service to complete Bomber Command's line-up of four-engine heavies.

One of Harris's immediate priorities was expansion. He had just over 500 aircraft available to him and so he immediately set about putting right the shortage of heavy bombers and to improve the efficiency of navigation aids and bombing techniques. Harris also knew that expansion would rely on having enough crews ready to take part in operations, which meant an increase in the training establishments with each group responsible for the training of its own bomber crews. This saw the creation of heavy conversion units (HCUs) to bridge the gap between the twin-engine Wellington used in training and the heavier four-engine bombers in operational service.

Harris was also keen to show doubters within the other services, as well as his own, that a bombing campaign, if conducted properly, would help bring an end to hostilities. He soon had enough assets to mount by far the biggest raid of the war and this took place against Cologne, Germany's third largest city, at the end of May 1942. It was the first part of Harris's 'Thousand-Bomber' plan and using all available resources, including aircraft and instructors from the command's many training units, 1,047 bombers were made available for the raid.

The first Thousand-Bomber raid was a success but a follow-up mass effort just two nights later, this time against Essen, was not. A third all-out effort was mounted against Bremen towards the end of June. This latest raid involved 1,067 bombers (including aircraft from Coastal Command and Army Co-Operation Command) and proved to be the RAF's largest raid of the war. Bomber Command had never before dispatched such a large and mixed force, nor would it do so again until the final weeks of the war.

These three Thousand-Bomber raids had shown how far Bomber Command had come in just a few months. Next came the improvement in navigation and bombing techniques, leading to the formation of the Path Finder Force (PFF) in August 1942. This idea had divided opinion within Bomber Command. While it was difficult to argue against having a trained force to find and mark targets, there was opposition to what was perceived by some to be an elite force within the command. Furthermore, group commanders were reluctant to give up their best crews. In the end, the initial composition of the PFF brought together squadrons from each of the bomber groups. Designated 8 (Pathfinder Force) Group, it would ultimately prove its worth; albeit at a heavy cost to its crews.

The introduction of the Pathfinders had coincided with the first American heavy bomber operations over Europe to give Bomber Command a daylight partner in a combined strategic bombing offensive against Nazi Germany. While the past year had been one of critical expansion, 1943 was to be a crucial year for Bomber Command as it was to be the first year that it could deliver the long-promised destructive power and with previously unheard of accuracy. The all-Canadian 6 (RCAF) Group was formed in Yorkshire at the beginning of the year and by the opening phase of the Battle of Berlin later in 1943 the group would be able to boast thirteen squadrons of the Royal Canadian Air Force (RCAF), all equipped with four-engine heavy bombers.

In addition to more bombers entering the combat arena, the technical war had also been developing at pace. Improvements in technology and the introduction of the Pathfinders had seen an improvement in overall bombing accuracy, three-fold at least, but as the RAF's technology and tactics continued to evolve, so did the Luftwaffe's. German night fighter crews were also achieving much success. The introduction of the *Lichtenstein* radar and the development of twin upward-firing cannons, known as *Schräge Musik*, had brought a new fear for the crews of Bomber Command. It was a combination that had turned the German night fighter into an extremely effective and potent weapon. Bomber Command losses continued to mount as the night war became a hard-fought and horrific campaign for both sides.

Bomber Command had now reorganized under a new base system. This consisted of a parent station, typically one of the

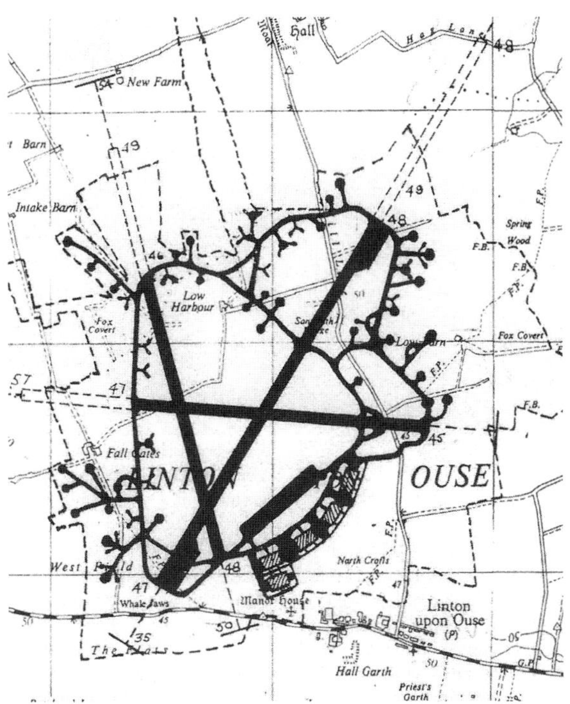

The standard layout of a bomber airfield during the Second World War was three hardened runways, constructed in a triangular A-pattern, with aircraft hard standings (usually enough for thirty-six heavy bombers), hangars and other buildings on a number of sites, all linked by a hardened perimeter track. The airfield shown here is Linton-on-Ouse. (RAF Linton-on-Ouse)

RAF's permanent pre-war airfields, with up to three sub-stations built as wartime airfields. These were numbered using two figures, the first giving the group to which the airfield belonged and the second the base itself. The group's training base was allocated the number one and the operational bases numbered thereafter. Using 6 (RCAF) Group as an example, its training base was Topcliffe, which became 61 (RCAF) Base with its sub-stations at Dalton, Dishforth and Wombleton, while Linton-on-Ouse, an operational airfield, became 62 (RCAF) Base, with its sub-stations at East Moor and Tholthorpe.

Bomber Command's campaign against the industrial Ruhr during 1943 was followed by the Battle of Hamburg and then the Battle of Berlin, the toughest and costliest of them all, which began in earnest in November 1943 and lasted until the end of March 1944. Sixteen major raids (more than 9,000 sorties) were flown against the Nazi capital for the loss of more than 500 aircraft. It was a particularly hard winter for the Halifax crews. Not only was it a long way to Berlin but the Merlin-powered Halifax II lacked the power to climb above bad weather and so there were occasions, particularly after suffering heavy losses, when the Halifax squadrons were stood down to leave

A Halifax of 1659 HCU undergoing maintenance at Topcliffe. The heavy conversion units played a vital part in supporting the bombing offensive against Nazi Germany by providing a continuous stream of trained crews to the operational squadrons. (AHB)

the Lancaster squadrons to continue the fight. The Halifax III, with Bristol Hercules radial engines, was an improvement and it was to become the most produced variant of the war but its bomb bay could not be modified to carry the larger bombs being designed and so it would be progressively outnumbered in frontline service as more Lancasters became available.

After Berlin came Bomber Command's heaviest loss in one night when a raid against Nuremberg on the last night of March 1944, involving nearly 800 aircraft, resulted in the loss of ninety-five bombers, including thirty-one of Yorkshire's Halifaxes. This marked the zenith for the Luftwaffe's night fighter force, the Nachtjagd, and Harris's belief that Germany could be defeated by sustained bombing alone had not proved to be the case.

As Bomber Command turned its attention to supporting the Allied landings in Europe, which took place on 6 June 1944, D-Day, its fortunes started to change. More and more operations were being flown by day as the Allies pushed further towards, and then into, Germany. With the war entering its final phase,

A spectacular image of a Halifax silhouetted against target indicators over Leipzig. (AHB)

and with Allied fighters gaining the upper hand, Bomber Command's losses started to fall as Germany's once invincible war machine became stretched across several fronts and the Luftwaffe suffered from a severe shortage of fuel.

In its six-year offensive Bomber Command had flown more than 360,000 operational sorties. The airfields of Yorkshire and County Durham had played a vital part in the Allied victory. Today, only a few have survived. Many have long reverted back to their pre-war agricultural days or are now used for other purposes. Fortunately, the legacy of most of these airfields lives on, told through the presence of memorials or in other ways by local volunteers who refuse to let the stories fade away.

I have chosen to tell the story of these airfields in two main parts. Part I covers the airfields of 4 Group, while Part II includes the airfields of 6 (RCAF) Group. When 6 (RCAF) Group formed at the beginning of 1943, a number of 4 Group's airfields were transferred across to the new Canadian group, in which case these are shown under 6 (RCAF) Group as this is the group they were serving under during the height of Bomber Command's strategic offensive of 1943/44. Part III is simply a catch-all to include Yorkshire's airfields that were part of the Bomber Command story but were not allocated to either of the county's main groups.

The format for each airfield is the same: its location; status; a brief history, focusing on the Second World War; how to find the airfield and what is there today; and a summary of its wartime units. Due to limited space only Bomber Command's wartime operational squadrons, HCUs and operational training units (OTUs) are shown. The summary includes the unit's code letters in brackets and after the dates, also in brackets, are the airfields from where the unit arrived and where it departed to. The aircraft type and mark operated by the unit is also shown, with dates where appropriate. Finally, to help summarize the story and for easy reference, I have included three appendices showing Bomber Command's operational order of battle in Yorkshire and County Durham at key points during the Second World War; at the beginning of hostilities (September 1939), the height of the Battle of Berlin (January 1944), and at the peak of its strength towards the end of the war (January 1945).

There is so much to tell but only limited space to do so. I hope you enjoy the book.

Peter Jacobs

Part I

Airfields of 4 Group

Re-formed on 1 April 1937 (it had previously existed for a year at the end of the First World War), 4 Group was initially headquartered at Mildenhall in Suffolk. Almost immediately, the headquarters relocated to Linton-on-Ouse in Yorkshire and by the outbreak of the Second World War the group had eight Whitley squadrons based at four airfields (Dishforth, Driffield, Leconfield and Linton-on-Ouse) under its Air Officer Commanding (AOC) Air Vice-Marshal Arthur Coningham.

4 Group flew its first operation of the war on the opening night of hostilities when ten Whitleys dropped propaganda leaflets over Germany, but it was not until the night of 19/20 March 1940 that the group's first raid on a land target took place when thirty Whitleys (from 10, 51, 77 and 102 Squadrons) joined twenty Hampdens of 5 Group to bomb the German seaplane base at Hörnum.

After German forces invaded France and the Low Countries in May, the gloves were off and with the threat of a German invasion of southern England becoming increasingly likely, 4 Group took part in attacks against the invasion ports across the Channel, as well as against oil targets in Germany. Its squadrons even flew raids against Berlin during August and September, although these were relatively small-scale and largely ineffective.

By now, 4 Group had re-located its headquarters to Heslington Hall, to the south-east of York, where it would remain for the rest of the war. During 1941, the group took part in attacks against the German battleships *Scharnhorst* and *Gneisenau* and helped to keep these mighty warships in harbour at Brest until February 1942 when they finally managed to break out in a high-speed dash through the Channel and back to their port at Kiel.

Bombing up a Whitley during the early phase of the Second World War. When hostilities broke out, 4 Group had only eight Whitley squadrons at four airfields. (via Ken Delve)

By early 1942, 4 Group had grown to eleven operational squadrons operating a mix of Halifaxes, Wellingtons and Whitleys. All but two of these were operating from seven different airfields in Yorkshire and County Durham: Croft, Dalton, Driffield, Leeming, Linton-on-Ouse, Middleton St George and Pocklington. Command of the group had passed to Roderick Carr and when Bomber Command ordered its all-out effort against Cologne at the end of May 1942, 4 Group was able to commit 147 aircraft to the Thousand Bomber force. According to *The Bomber Command War Diaries* by Martin Middlebrook and Chris Everitt, the breakdown of this figure gives 131 Halifaxes, nine Wellingtons and seven Whitleys, showing how the Halifax had now become the group's main frontline bomber.

When the Pathfinders formed, its new commander, Donald Bennett, was a former 4 Group squadron commander. Bennett had earlier commanded 77 Squadron (Whitleys) and 10 Squadron (Halifaxes) at Leeming. His new force was established with four squadrons, one from each of Bomber Command's main groups, with the Halifaxes of 35 Squadron being 4 Group's contribution.

Yorkshire had now become home to the Australians of 466 (RAAF) Squadron, initially a Wellington squadron but later to be equipped with Halifaxes and based at Leconfield. When the all-Canadian 6 (RCAF) Group formed in Yorkshire at the beginning of 1943 four of 4 Group's airfields – Leeming, Linton-on-Ouse, Middleton St George and Topcliffe – were transferred to the new group. 4 Group would also lose Marston Moor and its satellites (Acaster Malbis, Riccall and Rufforth) to 7 (Training) Group later in the year, but in return for these losses new airfields had opened at Breighton, Burn, Full Sutton, Holme-on-Spalding Moor, Lissett, Melbourne and Snaith.

4 Group continued to contribute large numbers of aircraft to Bomber Command's strategic offensives throughout 1943 – against the Ruhr, Hamburg and Berlin – after which it took part in the build-up to Operation *Overlord* and then supported the subsequent Allied breakout from Normandy towards Germany, including attacks against the German V-weapon sites in northern France. During this period Yorkshire became home to a second Australian Halifax squadron, 462 (RAAF) Squadron at Driffield, and Bomber Command's only Free French heavy bomber squadrons (346 and 347 Squadrons) based at Elvington.

The Halifax replaced the Whitley from 1941 to become the mainstay of 4 Group. The group would soon become an all-Halifax force. (Yorkshire Air Museum)

The Halifax proved a versatile aircraft and as the British Second Army advanced towards Arnhem, the squadrons of 4 Group were used to ferry large quantities of petrol across the Channel as an urgent re-supply. In one week, the Halifaxes ferried nearly half a million gallons of fuel.

In February 1945 Roderick Carr handed over as AOC to Air Vice-Marshal John Whitley, a well-known and experienced officer with 4 Group having commanded 149 Squadron, then Linton-on-Ouse and Lissett before taking command of 43 Base. 4 Group's last operation of the war was flown on 25 April 1945 against gun batteries on the Frisian island of Wangerooge, which controlled the approaches to the German naval ports of Bremen and Wilhelmshaven.

With the war over, 4 Group was transferred to Transport Command with its headquarters moving to Abingdon in Oxfordshire. According to figures from the Ministry of Defence, 4 Group flew a total of 61,577 operational sorties during the war, more than 40 per cent of which were flown during the group's operational peak in 1944.

Chapter 1

Acaster Malbis

Location – North Yorkshire, five miles south of York.
Status – Relief Landing Ground. 41 Base – sub-station of Marston Moor.

When talking about airfields of Yorkshire, the name of Acaster Malbis is rarely heard. Even in its heyday during the Second World War, there were fewer than 300 RAF personnel based at this smallest of stations.

It was not until late 1941 that work began on an area of land close to the River Ouse between the villages of Acaster Malbis and Acaster Selby to develop a grass airfield for the use of RAF fighters. By early 1942, the airfield was considered ready for opening and was allocated to Fighter Command as a satellite for nearby Church Fenton. Acaster Malbis was first used by 601 Squadron of the Royal Auxiliary Air Force, flying the American-built P39 Airacobra, but the squadron only remained for three months due to technical problems with the aircraft. Furthermore, the airfield had been built close to the western bank of the Ouse in an area full of dykes. Drainage was always a problem, particularly when the river was full or even flooded, causing the airfield to become waterlogged, as was the fog and mist caused by the river. Not surprisingly, it did not take long to discover that the airfield was not suitable for operations, particularly during any lengthy period of heavy rain and cold temperatures.

Considered unsuitable for further use by fighters, Acaster Malbis was transferred to Flying Training Command. From April 1942 until the end of the year, the airfield became home to Airspeed Oxfords but even training aircraft struggled to operate from the airfield and so, eventually, it was decided that Acaster

Acaster Malbis is one of the remotest of Yorkshire's wartime bomber airfields, with very few reminders of its past and most of the land having long reverted to agriculture. This is the north-west corner of the former airfield where part of the perimeter track can still be found. (Author)

Malbis was to undergo major reconstruction; it was either that or the RAF would have to move out altogether. The decision to upgrade the airfield was, to say the least, a strange one as it was never going to solve the problems that were essentially caused by the airfield's location. Nonetheless, construction work went ahead during 1943 rather than to give up on the site altogether and having earlier been rejected by two other commands, Acaster Malbis re-opened in November 1943 as a Class A bomber airfield and allocated to 4 Group.

The new airfield had three concrete runways with the main, 2,000 yards long, running from the north-east to the south-west. There were thirty-six hard standings for the dispersal of aircraft, three maintenance hangars and several other buildings, including enough domestic accommodation to house more than a thousand personnel. However, the airfield was never going to be suitable to sustain the operation of heavy bombers for any length of time, and so Acaster Malbis was only used as a relief landing ground for 4 Group's main training base at Marston Moor, now designated 41 Base, and its two satellites at Riccall and Rufforth.

Halifaxes soon became regular visitors to Acaster Malbis to practise circuits and approaches. During the latter period of the war the airfield was used by 91 Maintenance Unit for the storage of bombs before they were taken to the operational airfields nearby. From the end of 1944 the airfield was also home to 4 Group's Aircrew School for ground training and other non-flying aspects of training whilst crews waited for a posting to a squadron.

Towards the end of the war Acaster Malbis was transferred to 7 (Training) Group and when the war was over the MU moved out and flying ceased, after which the airfield closed in 1946. The site was, however, used for a number of years for the disposal of bombs and ammunition from the surrounding airfields in Yorkshire, a task that was not completed until the 1950s. The land was then sold, although private flying carried on into the 1980s. Large sections of the runways were then dug up and most of the airfield's buildings disappeared.

The former airfield of Acaster Malbis is one of the remotest and least easy to find of all Yorkshire's former wartime bomber airfields. There are very few reminders of its past with most of the land having long reverted to agriculture, although part of the land is used for light industry. The site of the former airfield can be found just over a mile to the south of the village of Acaster Malbis by heading south from the village, just on the western side of the River Ouse, along Mill Lane. Then continue south-westwards along Intake Lane until you reach the T-junction with Broad Lane. Turn left here in a southerly direction towards the village of Acaster Selby. York Saw Mill is immediately on your right, after which the lane takes a sharp right and then 400 yards or so later a sharp left. Almost immediately after you go round this left-hand bend you will see a gate and public footpath on your left. This is the north-west corner of the former airfield. The footpath follows the perimeter track, which is still evident, but do not take a car onto the perimeter track as the entrance gate can be locked at any time; there is space to park a car outside the entrance gate. If you continue south along the lane towards Acaster Selby, you will see Ebor Trucks on your left, which marks the area where hangars and buildings once stood, and continuing south along the lane takes you through what was the western part of the airfield, while Scaffold Dike and the River Ouse on the far side of the former airfield mark its eastern extremity.

Chapter 2

Breighton

Location – East Riding of Yorkshire, five miles to the north-east of Selby.
Status – Satellite airfield. 44 Base – sub-station of Holme-on-Spalding Moor.

Not one of the RAF's pre-war airfields, Breighton's early life as a bomber station differed to others in Yorkshire as it was with 1 Group that the airfield first served rather than the county's other airfields of 4 Group.

It was during 1941 that construction work was carried out on land between the villages of Breighton, from which the airfield takes its name, and Bubwith. Although built as a bomber airfield with three hardened runways, the runways met at a common intersection rather than being of the standard A-type design. The main runway was aligned approximately east–west, while a second runway ran from the south-west to the north-east and the third ran almost north–south. The eastern extension of the main east–west runway took the runway as far as the B1228. Other than that, the airfield was built as normal, with a perimeter track and thirty-six hard standings for aircraft dispersal. The technical site, which included two hangars, was in the north-west corner of the airfield, near the village of Gunby, while a third hangar was on the southern boundary and adjacent to the original southern threshold of the north-south runway.

Breighton opened in January 1942 as a satellite of Holme-on-Spalding Moor and immediately allocated to 1 Group, Bomber Command. The first resident unit to move in was the Australian 460 (RAAF) Squadron, then equipped with the Wellington IV. The crews immediately moved in to the new airfield from their former base at Molesworth in Huntingdonshire. The squadron

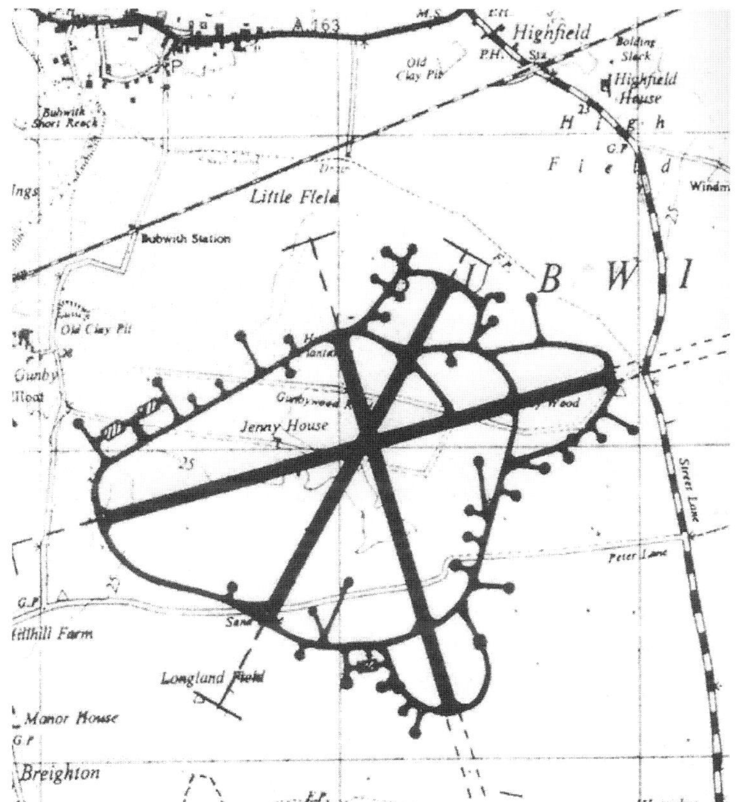

Somewhat unusually, the runways at Breighton met at a common intersection rather than being of the standard A-type design. Other than that the airfield had been constructed to the standard bomber design. (via Ken Delve)

had been formed from C Flight of 458 Squadron just a few weeks before and after settling down to its new home flew its first operations from the airfield on the night of 12/13 March 1942. Five aircraft joined Bomber Command's Main Force to attack the port of Emden in north-west Germany. One Wellington failed to return.

The squadron suffered its first loss from Breighton at the end of April but the Wellingtons were not destined to stay long as by the summer they were gradually being phased out of operational service in favour of the new four-engine heavier bombers being introduced. In August, the squadron began taking delivery of the Halifax II four-engine heavy bomber but the squadron never flew these operationally. The Halifaxes made up the squadron's conversion flight, which immediately moved to Holme-on-Spalding Moor, another bomber airfield of 1 Group.

The following month the conversion flight returned to Breighton under the command of Wing Commander K W Kaufman DFC. Its Halifaxes were replaced by a handful of Manchesters and Lancasters, and the flight then merged with another conversion flight to become 1656 HCU, which officially formed at Breighton in October 1942.

The HCU did not stay long and the following month moved to its permanent base at Lindholme. 460 Squadron, meanwhile, had been busy converting to the Lancaster and was ready to resume operations on the night of 22/23 November. The target was Stuttgart but conditions were not great for bombing. A mix of cloud and ground haze made marking difficult and most bombs fell outside the city centre. Amongst the five Lancasters lost on the raid was an aircraft of 460 Squadron.

The following month, the squadron was handed over to Wing Commander J F Dilworth DFC who held the reigns until February when he was replaced by Wing Commander C E Martin. The squadron then moved out to Binbrook in Lincolnshire, one of 1 Group's main airfields.

One Lancaster serving with 460 at this time was W4783 'AR-G George' – a Mark I built by Metropolitan-Vickers Limited in Manchester and delivered to Breighton in October 1942. The aircraft soon flew its first op and went on to fly thirty-four missions from Breighton before 'G-George' was transferred to its new Lincolnshire home, from where it went on to complete ninety operations with the squadron. Given the high losses being suffered by the Aussies at that time, the chances of 'G-George' completing a further ten ops to become a centurion were considered unlikely and so the aircraft was retired from ops in 1944 and later flown to Australia to be preserved. It has since been on display at the museum at the Australian War Memorial in Canberra.

With the departure of 460 Squadron, Breighton was transferred to 4 Group. That same month, June 1943, saw the arrival of Halifaxes of 78 Squadron from Linton-on-Ouse to free up space

Halifax of 78 Squadron. The squadron moved to Breighton in June 1943 and the airfield remained its home for the rest of the war. (AHB)

at Linton for the Canadians, and Breighton would remain 78's home for the rest of the war.

78 Squadron had arrived at Breighton just in time to join Bomber Command's main campaign against the industrial Ruhr and so there was little time for the crews to settle in. The squadron also took part in the command's major raid against the Nazi V-weapons secret research establishment at Peenemünde on the Baltic coast on the night of 17/18 August 1943. Twenty-three of its aircraft took part in the raid, with all returning safely. However, the squadron was not so fortunate a few nights later, on 23/24 August, when taking part in a raid against Berlin. Five of its aircraft were lost that night, three of which fell to enemy night fighters and the other two collided over Yorkshire after being ordered to divert to Leconfield because of bad weather at Breighton.

For 78 Squadron, it had been the costliest night of the war so far but its worst night was yet to come when six of its Halifaxes were lost during a raid against Berlin on the night of 24/25 March 1944. Five aircraft had fallen to the guns of night fighters while the sixth crashed in Norfolk on its way home. Twenty-two lives were lost. It was the last raid against Berlin of the campaign but it would be a while before things would improve. Three more squadron aircraft were lost on the disastrous Nuremberg raid the following week.

By now, the squadron had replaced its Halifax IIs with the improved Mark III. The squadron was then under the command of Wing Commander Markland, the first wireless operator to command a bomber squadron, and soon became heavily involved in the build-up to the Allied landings in Normandy as part of Operation *Overlord*. Then, during the early hours of 6 June 1944, just ahead of the first troops going ashore, the squadron joined others from 4 Group to make up an attacking force of 124 aircraft tasked with bombing the coastal gun battery at Mont Fleury.

There was to be no rest during the weeks ahead and the following night, 7/8 June, the squadron made up part of a force of nearly 200 Halifaxes joining more than a hundred Lancasters to carry out further attacks against key targets in an attempt to stop the Germans reinforcing the Normandy area. Amongst the targets were several railway yards, including one at Juvisy, and although the attack was successful, 78 Squadron lost four of its aircraft during the raid. The German night fighters had been able to get amongst the raiders and twenty-eight of the attacking force of 337 aircraft had been lost (more than 8 per cent).

78 Squadron lost a total of eight aircraft during June 1944. It was a key month of the war but it had cost the lives of thirty-eight airmen from Breighton. With the Allies then safely ashore, the squadron supported the subsequent breakout from the Normandy beaches. Things would now improve as the Allies gained air superiority over north-west Europe. Losses from Breighton reduced but they would not go away. One unfortunate example occurred in October when two of the squadron's aircraft collided over Holland, killing all on board.

During the final weeks of hostilities the squadron took delivery of the Halifax VI, but only in small numbers. The war was all but over and the squadron's last operational sorties were flown on 25 April 1945 against gun batteries on the island of Wangerooge.

At the end of the war, along with the other bomber squadrons of 4 Group, 78 Squadron was transferred to Transport Command and converted to Dakotas for transport duties in the Mediterranean and Middle East. Breighton then closed to flying and the land gradually reverted to agriculture, although the site was home to Bloodhound missiles during the early 1960s and used to store Thor missiles before the airfield finally closed in 1964.

The airfield can be found on the north-east corner of Breighton village, to the south of the village of Bubwith, between the

Part of Breighton is still active today and used by the York Flying School as well as by the classic aircraft collection of the Real Aeroplane Company and the Real Aeroplane Club. The crew room (far right) is a former wartime building on what was part of the technical site. A memorial dedicated to all who served at Breighton and gave their lives during the Second World War stands between the crew room and the hangar. (Author)

eastern bank of the River Derwent and the B1228 Street Lane. The south-west part of the old airfield is still active today. One grass runway runs just off an east-west direction along the line of one of the former taxiways and is used for private flying by the York Flying School as well as by the classic aircraft collection of the Real Aeroplane Company and the Real Aeroplane Club, an active flying club whose members own and operate many unusual, classic and ex-military aircraft. The crew room used today is in a former wartime building on what was then part of the technical site. A memorial dedicated to all who served at Breighton and gave their lives during the Second World War stands between the crew room and the hangar. This part of the airfield can be accessed from Gunby Road, which connects the villages of Breighton and Bubwith, but visits can only be made with prior permission. It is, nonetheless, well worth a visit.

There are several other reminders of this former wartime bomber airfield, including an old wartime T2 hangar used today for agricultural storage. It can be found at the western extremity of the airfield, about half a mile south of Bubwith off Gunby

The eastern end of the main runway has survived, much of which is now covered by buildings of the industrial estate. (Author)

Road just after the turn-off to Gunbywood Road. The eastern extremity of the main east-west runway has survived and in recent years was used by light aircraft for crop-spraying. Much of this runway is now covered by buildings of the industrial estate but parts of the former runway, as well as outlines of the

In the churchyard at Bubwith is a memorial to 78 Squadron. It was unveiled in 1986 by Sir Guy Lawrence, who had commanded the squadron during 1943/44. (Author)

hardened areas and parts of the taxiways and hard standings, can still be seen. This part of the old airfield is accessible from the B1228 Street Lane at the eastern end, which runs south from the main A163 that passes through Bubwith village. In the churchyard at Bubwith is a memorial to 78 Squadron. It was unveiled in 1986 by Sir Guy Lawrence, who had commanded the squadron during 1943/44.

Summary of units based at Breighton during the Second World War

460 (RAAF) Squadron (UV & AR) – 4 Jan 42 (Molesworth) – 13 May 43 (Binbrook)
Wellington IV (Jan – Aug 42)
Halifax II (Aug – Oct 42)
Lancaster I/III (Oct 42 – May 43)

1656 HCU – Oct 42 (Formed) – Nov 42 (Lindholme)
Manchester I
Lancaster I

78 Squadron (EY) – 16 Jun 43 (Linton-on-Ouse) – 20 Sep 45 (moved overseas)
Halifax II (Jun 43 – Jan 44)
Halifax III (Jan 44 – Apr 45)
Halifax VI (Apr – Jul 45)

CHAPTER 3

Burn

Location – North Yorkshire, three miles south-west of Selby. Status: Operational airfield.

Not far from the airfield of Breighton is the former Bomber Command airfield of Burn, which today lies amongst farmers' fields to the south-west of Selby. Burn is another airfield to have been built during the early years of the Second World War.

Contained by a number of communications routes – the Selby Canal, the main A19 Selby–York road and the Doncaster–Selby railway line – a major factor when determining the airfield's location and size, work to construct the new airfield commenced in late 1941. The airfield was built to the standard design with three hardened runways; the main, nearly 2,000 yards long, ran in a near north–south direction parallel to the railway line, while the two intersecting runways were each around 1,400 yards long. A hardened perimeter track linked the runways with thirty-six aircraft hard standings and three maintenance hangars, and there was enough accommodation for up to 2,000 personnel.

Burn officially opened as an airfield of 4 Group in November 1942, although it had already been used for a brief period by Liberators of 1653 HCU, which moved in from Polebrook during the summer. There had been an idea at that time to equip part of Bomber Command's 1 Group with the American-built Consolidated B-24 Liberator but the plan never came to fruition and so the HCU was disbanded just a few weeks later.

The first squadron to conduct operations from Burn was the Canadian 431 (Iroquois) Squadron RCAF, which formed in November 1942. By the end of the year the Canadians had taken delivery of the first Wellington X bombers and after completing its work-up the squadron commenced operations on the night of 5/6 March 1943 when three of its aircraft took part in a raid against Essen.

The squadron soon built up in size and took part in an all-out effort against Dortmund on the night of 23/24 May. This latest raid took place after a short period of rest for the crews of Bomber Command's Main Force. 617 Squadron had just carried out the legendary Dams Raid but it was now time to resume the strategic bombing campaign against the industrial Ruhr. The mixed force of Lancasters, Halifaxes, Stirlings, Wellingtons and Mosquitos – a total of 826 aircraft – sent to Dortmund that night was the largest force since the Thousand Bomber raids a year before, and the largest force to attack a single target during this latest campaign. The raid was a success. Many industrial buildings and factories were hit during the attack, so much so that Bomber Command was able to leave this target alone for another year.

Amongst the many personal stories from the Dortmund raid that night is the extraordinary tale of 21-year-old Sergeant Stuart 'Scotty' Sloan, an English bomb aimer serving with the Canadian squadron at Burn. Having completed its attack, Sloan's Wellington had become coned by searchlights and was badly damaged after being hit several times by flak. Despite taking evasive action, the pilot could not shake off the searchlights and remained under sustained heavy fire. The situation had become so critical that the pilot ordered the crew to bale out, but by the time Sloan was about to leave the aircraft he realized that two of the crew members had not heard the order and were still on board.

With the pilot having already left the aircraft, Sloan took the controls and managed to get the Wellington under control. Still harassed by flak and searchlights, he carried out a number of manoeuvres to escape the enemy defences. Then, once they were out of immediate danger, he set course for home. Sloan then discussed with his two colleagues whether they should abandon the aircraft or not, but they all decided to stay.

Inside the Wellington, a gale was blowing through the fuselage from where the escape hatch had been left open. It could not be closed and the rear turret door was also open. The lights had been extinguished, making it very dark inside the fuselage, but the navigator, Sergeant George Parslow, still managed to plot a course for home. Throughout the return flight Parslow and the wireless operator, 22-year-old Flying Officer John Bailey, assisted Sloan in every way they could and eventually the badly damaged bomber was back over the Norfolk coast. They again discussed whether Parslow and Bailey should abandon the aircraft while Sloan attempted a landing, but they both decided to stay. Then, having found an airfield, Sloan nursed the aircraft down to make an emergency landing. It was a remarkable piece of flying.

The Wellington had landed at Cranwell in Lincolnshire. In appalling circumstances, Sloan, Parslow and Bailey had displayed great courage, determination and fortitude of the highest order, for which Sloan was awarded the Conspicuous Gallantry Medal (CGM), while Parslow received the Distinguished Flying Medal (DFM) and Bailey the Distinguished Flying Cross (DFC). When the facts unfolded about the events that night, Sloan's senior officers were so impressed that he was instantly commissioned and posted for pilot training; he later returned to Bomber Command as a Halifax pilot and survived the war, adding a DFC to his CGM. Unfortunately, though, George Parslow and John Bailey were not so lucky. After their ordeal of the Dortmund raid that night they were transferred to the crew of the squadron commander, Wing Commander John Coverdale, but the crew were reported missing just a month later.

431 Squadron moved out to Tholthorpe in July 1943, leaving Burn non-operational for the time being. Although relatively inactive, the airfield remained open and was frequently used by the Halifaxes of the HCUs at Marston Moor and Riccall, either as a diversion airfield or as a relief landing ground for the training of bomber crews. Burn was also used during early 1944 by Austers of 658 and 659 Squadrons, both air observation squadrons working with the army, their role generally being to work with artillery units to carry out aerial observation. Both squadrons moved out again by the end of April.

Burn was now under the command of Group Captain David Marwood-Elton DFC and returned to operations in February 1944, during the height of the Battle of Berlin, when Halifax IIIs of the newly formed 578 Squadron moved in from Snaith. Although the nucleus of the squadron had formed the previous

Twenty-two year old Cyril Barton, a pilot serving with 578 Squadron, was posthumously awarded the Victoria Cross for his courage during the disastrous Nuremberg raid on the night of 30/31 March 1944. Barton was the only member of a Halifax crew to be awarded Britain's highest award for gallantry. (AHB)

month from crews of 51 Squadron, others had joined 578 from other squadrons within 4 Group; an example being 22-year-old Pilot Officer Cyril Barton, who arrived with his crew from Breighton having initially been posted to 78 Squadron.

578 Squadron was under the command of 26-year-old Wing Commander David Wilkerson DFC, known to his crews as 'Wingco Wilkie'. Under his fine leadership it did not take the squadron long to work up to full strength. By mid-March it was able to send in excess of a dozen aircraft on raids. However, one of 578's aircraft failed to return from a raid against Frankfurt on the night of 22/23 March. It was one of seven Halifaxes lost by Bomber Command that night and flying as the second pilot was Burn's station commander, David Marwood-Elton. Fortunately, the crew survived to be taken as prisoners of war but in Marwood-Elton the Germans had captured a difficult character. As the Senior British Officer at a POW camp at Barthe, he was arrested by the Germans after issuing an order to his fellow prisoners to acknowledge only military salutes and not the Nazi salute. This was considered by his captors to be an act of mutiny. Marwood-Elton was detained and subsequently faced a trial. Unsurprisingly, he was found guilty and sent to a

prison in Stettin, although he subsequently returned to Barthe where he would be liberated at the end of the war.

Meanwhile, back at Burn, Marwood-Elton had been replaced as station commander by Group Captain J Warburton. 578 Squadron was still increasing in size and by the Nuremberg raid on the night of 30/31 March 1944 it was able to send twelve aircraft. One was LK797 'LK-E Excalibur', flown by Cyril Barton on his nineteenth op.

Barton got airborne just after 9.15 p.m. The clear sky and bright moonlight were early indications that it was going to be a difficult night but for most of the transit to the target the crew had been fortunate to avoid any trouble. The first they became aware of immediate danger was when they spotted pale red parachute flares, dropped by Junkers Ju 88 night fighters to mark the position of the bomber stream. The sky was clear and the crew watched in horror as night fighters suddenly appeared. One by one their colleagues were picked off. They knew it would soon be their turn but they were now on the final leg towards the target and there was to be no turning back. Suddenly, two night fighters appeared in front, attacking head-on, just as cannon shells ripped through the Halifax; puncturing fuel tanks and knocking out the aircraft's rear turret and all of its communications, while setting the starboard inner engine on fire. Barton threw the aircraft into a hard evasive manoeuvre just as a Ju 88 passed close by. Corkscrewing as hard as he dare, he took the Halifax down. For a while, it seemed the danger had passed but no sooner had Barton resumed his course towards Nuremberg than the Halifax was attacked once more. Shells again raked the fuselage for a second time. The Ju 88 was momentarily seen to break off its attack but it was soon back again, scoring more hits on the crippled bomber before eventually turning away.

Undaunted, Barton again resumed his course for Nuremberg. He was finally able to assess the damage to his aircraft, only to find that three of his crew members had gone. Unable to communicate with their skipper, and with the bomber repeatedly under heavy attack while corkscrewing towards the ground, the navigator, bomb aimer and wireless operator had all abandoned the aircraft to become prisoners of war. Now in a somewhat desperate situation, Barton contemplated what to do next. With a crippled bomber, one engine out, leaking fuel, the rear turret out of action, no communications or navigational assistance, and with three of his crew missing, he would have been fully justified in aborting his mission. Barton, instead, decided to press on to the target with just his two air gunners, Sergeants Freddie Brice and Harry Wood, and his flight engineer, Sergeant Maurice Trousdale, left on board.

The four airmen struggled on. By working together and using the stars to navigate, they eventually reached the target and completed their attack before finally turning for home. Remarkably, they managed to keep out of further trouble as Barton nursed the crippled Halifax back towards safety. It was an outstanding feat of airmanship for a pilot so young. The crew, however, were still not out of danger and although Barton was satisfied they had coasted-in somewhere over eastern England, they still had to find somewhere to land. It was just before 6 a.m. and still dark but the Halifax was now desperately short of fuel. As Barton eased the bomber down, he was all too aware that the remaining engines were about to give up. With his three crew colleagues braced behind the aircraft's rear spar, he was all alone in the cockpit. Visibility was extremely poor and suddenly a row of terraced houses appeared in front. Yanking the control column back in a desperate attempt to hurdle the obstacles before him, a wing first clipped the chimneys before the Halifax came crashing down, demolishing everything in its way.

The Halifax had come down in the yard of Ryhope colliery in County Durham. One miner was killed in the wreckage. Remarkably, though, the three crew members braced in the rear of the fuselage had survived; they were all to later receive the DFM. Fortunately for them, the rear section of the aircraft had broken away on impact. The forward section, however, still with the gallant young pilot inside, was a wreck of twisted metal. Barton was pulled from the wreckage and rushed to hospital but he died from his injuries the following day. A few weeks later came the announcement of the posthumous award of the Victoria Cross to Cyril Barton. It was 4 Group's only VC of the war and the only award to a member of a Halifax crew. Barton's citation, which appeared in the *London* Gazette on Friday 23 June 1944, concludes:

In gallantly completing his last mission in the face of almost impossible odds, this officer displayed unsurpassed courage and devotion to duty.

Of the twelve Halifaxes that had taken off from Burn that night, one had to return early because of an engine problem and landed elsewhere, while another failed to return having, it seems, been shot down over the target. Only one Halifax managed to make it all the way back to Burn. The eight others all landed at other bomber airfields in England, although one crash-landed killing six members of the crew.

The disastrous raid against Nuremberg was yet another costly reminder that large-scale raids deep into Nazi Germany were still extremely hazardous and often resulted in heavy losses. Unfortunately for all the bomber crews based at Burn during the long and hard winter of 1943/44, they had come up against the Luftwaffe's night fighter force at the peak of its effectiveness.

In July 1944, the popular David Wilkerson handed over command of 578 to Wing Commander A G T James and went off to attend a flying course at Hullavington. Wilkerson had completed forty-seven operational sorties and had added a Distinguished Service Order (DSO) to his DFC. Just weeks later, he was on a visit to Rednal in Shropshire. He and four course colleagues had made the journey in an American-built Martin Baltimore, a light bomber, but tragedy struck on 16 September after the aircraft had taken off for the return journey to Hullavington. Wilkerson was flying as a passenger and the aircraft was seen to hit the ground beyond some trees just moments after take-off. It appears the aircraft may have suffered an engine failure but it has also been suggested that the tail-locking mechanism for the rudder was still applied, preventing its full movement. David Wilkerson DSO DFC was aged twenty-seven. At the request of his family, his body was returned to Burn for burial in Selby Cemetery by members of the squadron that he had so proudly commanded and led with distinction. Wilkerson's burial took place four days after his death and was attended by 4 Group's most senior officers, including the AOC, Air Vice-Marshal Roderick Carr, the commander of 41 Base, Air Commodore J L Kirby, the station commander at Burn, Group

Captain J Warburton, and 578's new squadron commander, Wing Commander James.

578 Squadron continued to take part in most of Bomber Command's major efforts until the final weeks of the war. By then, command of the squadron had been handed over to Wing Commander E L Hancock. The last operational sorties were flown from Burn on 13 March 1945 when fourteen aircraft made up part of a large Bomber Command force of more than 300 Halifaxes from 4 and 6 Groups sent to the industrial city of Wuppertal in the Ruhr. No aircraft were lost, although cloud had covered the target area making accurate bombing difficult with many bombs falling in the eastern suburb of Barmen.

Two days later the squadron disbanded. The war was all but over. During its brief existence of just fifteen months 578 Squadron had flown more than 2,700 operational sorties against more than a hundred targets and dropped nearly 10,000 tons of bombs. Two of its aircraft each flew more than a hundred ops. When taking into account the fact that only four Halifaxes survived long enough to become centurions, to have two of these aircraft on the same squadron is remarkable and marks an outstanding achievement by all those involved. One, LW587, flew as the squadron's 'LK-V' and 'LK-A' and completed its one hundredth op on the raid against Bergkamen on the night of 3/4 March 1945. Its final total was 104 ops. The second aircraft, MZ527, went one op better as 'LK-W' and 'LK-D'. Coincidentally, it also became a centurion on the Bergkamen raid but both of these legendary Halifaxes were soon to be struck off charge, MZ527 before the war was even over. It was hardly the end they deserved. One of the other two Halifax centurions was LV937, known as 'Expensive Babe', which also served with 578 Squadron as 'LK-X' and 'LK-R' until April 1944, when it was transferred to Snaith where it went on to complete its one hundredth operational sortie.

With the disbandment of 578 Squadron flying ceased at Burn. Like a number of Bomber Command's airfields during the Second World War, its operational existence had been brief. At its peak, Burn had been home to 2,500 service personnel. The land was briefly retained by the government after the war and used for the disposal of various pieces of military equipment.

Remarkably, this former wartime airfield has survived and can be found to the south-west of Selby on the eastern side of

Looking west across the former wartime airfield, now home to Burn Gliding Club. (Author)

the A19 at the small village of Burn. It is bounded to the north by the Selby Canal, with Common Lane marking the northern extremity of the airfield, and to the east by the main railway line. The layout of the airfield is almost as it was more than seventy years ago and its connection with flying lives on through the Burn Gliding Club, which operates on the airfield from its modern brick building on the western part of the site where one of the wartime hangars once stood. It can be accessed from Park Lane, which runs behind the Wheatsheaf pub and opposite the church on the A19, at the end of a row of new houses.

It is possible to visit the gliding club, although on non-flying days the gate is locked to vehicles. You can, however, gain pedestrian access to the site. You can follow the perimeter track to the former runways, which are now used for gliding and so permission will be required on flying days; if in doubt, stick to the perimeter track. Following the perimeter track from the club to the right, southwards, it takes you to the south-western threshold of Runway 07/25. Heading along the old runway in an east-northeast direction takes you to Runway 33/15. Because it headed into the prevailing westerly wind, this runway was

Two memorials, one to 431 (Iroquois) Squadron and the other to 578 Squadron (on the left of the two), can be found opposite the Wheatsheaf Inn on the A19 near the entrance to Burn Gliding Club. (Author)

regularly in use during the war but take-offs on 33 were not favoured by the Halifax crews when taking off in a fully laden bomber; rising ground at the north-west end of the airfield being the reason why. Following this runway towards the south-east takes you to the intersection of Runway 01/19, which runs parallel to the railway line.

The main entrance to the wartime airfield was on Burn Lane and this is where the majority of domestic and administrative buildings once stood. The bomb dump was on the northern extremity of the airfield near the Selby Canal. The airfield's wartime buildings, including the control tower, were demolished many years ago. Considering there were once well over 200 separate buildings, the only obvious land mark that has survived from the wartime days is the old water tower. Opposite the Wheatsheaf Inn on the A19 there are two memorials to all those who served with 431 (Iroquois) Squadron and 578 Squadron at Burn during the Second World War.

Summary of units based at Burn during the Second World War

1653 HCU – Jun 42 (Polebrook) – Oct 42 (Disbanded)
B-24 Liberator

431 (Iroquois) Squadron RCAF (SE) – 11 Nov 42 (Formed) – 14 Jul 43 (Tholthorpe)
Wellington X

578 Squadron (LK) – 6 Feb 44 (Snaith) – 15 Apr 45 (Disbanded)
Halifax III

Chapter 4

Carnaby (Bridlington)

Location – East Riding of Yorkshire, two miles south-west of Bridlington.
Status – Emergency runway for Bomber Command.

Built on Carnaby Moor, this was another site developed as an airfield during the latter period of the Second World War. Work did not begin until 1943, but unlike Yorkshire's other bomber airfields, Carnaby was never going to

Because Carnaby was expected to be available to crews in all kinds of weather its facilities included FIDO, an ingenious method of dealing with fog based around a network of pipes filled with fuel and laid along the edges of the runway. When the fuel was set alight it lifted the fog high enough to allow aircraft to land. (AHB)

accommodate operational squadrons or training units. It was, instead, to serve as an emergency landing ground for Bomber Command, for use by returning bombers that had been severely damaged and unable to return to their home base. It was one of three airfields used for this purpose in eastern England during the war, the others being at Manston in Kent and at Woodbridge in Suffolk.

Carnaby opened in March 1944 and allocated to 4 Group. Because of its role the airfield had not been constructed to the standard bomber layout but had instead been built with just one long hardened runway constructed of special bitumen, 3,000 yards long and 250 yards wide (much longer and five times the width of a normal runway), with a grass extension of 500 yards at each end. Being such a wide runway, it was effectively divided into three lanes. The left lane was kept clear for the highest state of emergency and was made available to crews that were unable to make any form of radio contact with the airfield, while the two other lanes were allocated by the control tower according to the need at the time, with there being enough width to land two aircraft side-by-side. A short taxiway connected the

Many bomber crews were grateful that Carnaby was available, including this Lancaster crew of 100 Squadron. (via Ken Delve)

runway with some aircraft hard standings on a dispersal loop at its western end rather than being situated around the airfield. There were no hangars or permanent technical buildings; it was not that type of airfield.

As Carnaby was expected to cope with all kinds of incidents, every type of emergency service was available at the airfield. More than 500 personnel were based there at any one time, living in very basic accommodation, with overall administration for their welfare provided by Lissett.

As an emergency airfield, Carnaby had been planned well. Being so close to the east coast meant the airfield was ideally situated for bombers returning from raids across the North Sea that were, for whatever reason, unable to land at their home airfields in eastern England. Aircraft could approach from the sea and the long and wide runway would have been a most welcome sight for any crew in an emergency.

The runway was expected to be available to crews in all kinds of weather and so Carnaby's facilities included FIDO (standing for 'Fog Investigation and Dispersal Operation, but sometimes referred to as 'Fog Intense Dispersal Operation' or 'Fog, Intense Dispersal Of'), an ingenious method of dealing with fog or poor visibility, both quite common in eastern England. The system was based around a network of pipes filled with fuel and laid along the edges of the runway. In the case of poor visibility, the fuel was ignited and the effect was to lift the fog up to a height of around 300 feet, high enough to enable aircraft to land. As one of only two Yorkshire airfields to be equipped with FIDO (the other being Melbourne), one of Carnaby's busiest days was at the end of January 1945 when sixty-five American bombers were diverted to the airfield because of bad weather at their home base.

From the day it opened, the emergency airfield of Carnaby proved its worth and was regularly used by aircraft of both Bomber Command and the American Eighth Air Force, with some 1,500 landings recorded by the end of the war. With hostilities over, the airfield closed. It was then left in disrepair for a number of years but was always considered a useful asset and so there was no rush to dispose of the site. Carnaby was then given a new lease of life during the early 1950s when it was used as a relief landing ground for Driffield, and then during the

Looking east-north-east along what was the former runway at Carnaby, now a road leading through the main industrial estate. It is appropriately named Lancaster Road. (Author)

late 1950s and early 1960s, when it was used as a Thor missile site before Carnaby closed for the last time in 1963. During the 1970s part of the runway and perimeter track was used as a racing track for motorcycles, after which the site was developed as an industrial estate with the former runway becoming a road. Other reminders, of which there were few in the first place, have long disappeared.

The former airfield can be found three miles to the south-west of Bridlington and just a mile to the south-west of the village of Carnaby. When travelling south from Bridlington along the A165 Kingsgate, pass the golf course and a caravan park on your left, and 400 yards later you will come to a roundabout. Turn right into Moor Lane and after 400 yards you will see Carnaby Industrial Estate on your left. Turn left into the estate along the appropriately named Lancaster Road and you are now driving along the length of the former runway.

CHAPTER 5

Cottam

Location – East Riding of Yorkshire, five miles north of Driffield.
Status – Satellite of Driffield.

The airfield of Cottam, named after the village nearby, was developed at the outbreak of the Second World War as a satellite of Driffield and part of 4 Group, Bomber Command. Within a year, it had been completed to the normal bomber standard with three hardened runways (the main being 1,800 yards long and running east-west), a perimeter track, one hangar, aircraft hard standings to accommodate up to twenty-four aircraft and temporary accommodation for around 1,000 personnel.

Although Cottam was ready to accept aircraft from September 1940, no bomber units moved in. Wind patterns were often unpredictable and being built on a hill with difficult access to the site, it can be seen why this airfield was not used nor developed further. The only known period of use was for a short period during the autumn of 1940, when the airfield first opened, when aircraft of 4 Group's Target Towing Flight used Cottam after their home base at Driffield had been severely damaged during an enemy attack.

Cottam was used mainly as a maintenance unit during the latter period of the war, but with hostilities over, the airfield was abandoned. The runways and perimeter track were dug up during the 1970s and 1980s, and the former control tower demolished. Today, very few reminders of this former airfield remain.

The site of this former wartime airfield can be found five miles north of the town of Driffield on the western side of the

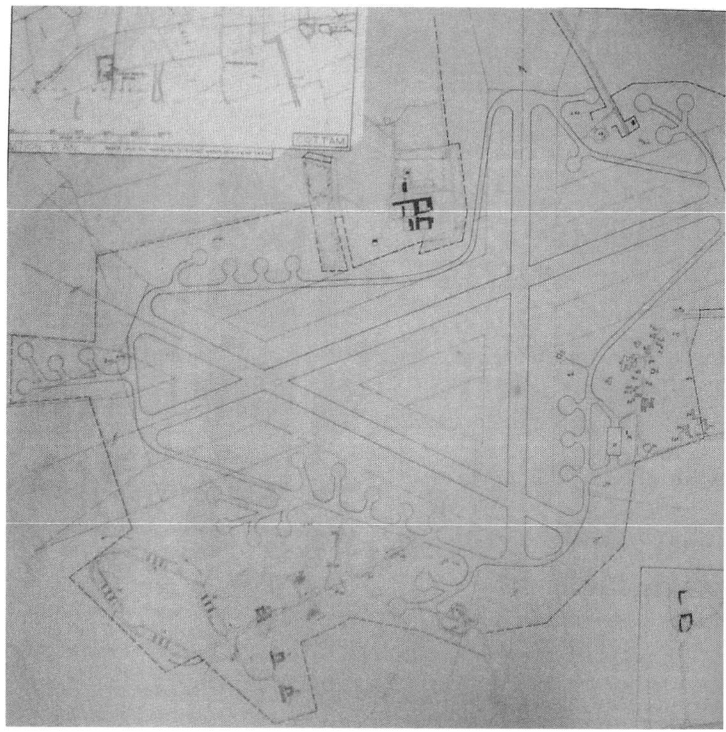

Layout of Cottam as it would have appeared in 1944. Although built to the standard bomber design, its location on a hill with unpredictable wind patterns and the lack of easy access to the site were all reasons why this airfield was little used. (via Ken Delve)

B1249. When travelling south along the B1249 from the village of Langtoft towards Driffield, continue past the turn-off left (Kilham Road) and after about a mile, and shortly before the turning left to the village of Kilham called York Road, there is a turning right along a minor lane. This lane, which runs west before heading north, takes you through the site of the former airfield, although the land has long reverted to agriculture.

CHAPTER 6

Driffield (Eastburn)

Location – East Riding of Yorkshire, two miles south-west of Driffield.
Status – Operational airfield. HQ 43 Base.

One of Yorkshire's oldest airfields, and the furthest east of the county's pre-Second World War airfields, is Driffield. Its origins date back to the First World War when the airfield was called Eastburn, after the village to its west, when it was used by the Royal Flying Corps as a training aerodrome, as well as a relief landing ground for Home Defence squadrons. After the war the aerodrome was improved, but there were no military plans for the site during the 1920s and so it was not until ten years later that the land was surveyed and found suitable for development as one of a dozen main RAF airfields in the north-east.

The new airfield, now called Driffield, was constructed to a standard bomber grass airfield design and opened in July 1936. Initially part of 3 Group, Bomber Command, the first occupants were two squadrons of Vickers Virginia biplane bombers. For the next two years, squadrons came and went, and by the outbreak of the Second World War Driffield had been transferred to 4 Group.

When hostilities broke out, Driffield was home to Whitleys of 102 and 77 Squadrons, two squadrons that would make Yorkshire their home for most of the war. The first operational sorties were flown from the airfield as early as the night of 4/5 September 1939 when three Whitleys went Nickelling over the Ruhr.

With bombing of the German mainland prohibited for the time being, the Nickelling sorties went on throughout the period

Whitley of 102 Squadron pictured at Driffield during 1940. (IWM)

of the so-called Phoney War, and by using airfields in northern France the Whitleys were able to extend these sorties further across Europe. One unusual incident, involving an aircraft of 77 Squadron, took place on the night of 15/16 March 1940, while returning from dropping propaganda leaflets over Warsaw. It had been the second visit by Bomber Command to the Polish capital but was the first for the squadron. The Whitley V, with its crew of five, was captained by 24-year-old Flight Lieutenant Brian Tomlin, a pre-war pilot from Surrey.

Tomlin and his crew had left Driffield with another Whitley five days earlier to operate from Metz in the north-east of France. But a period of bad weather – snow, sleet, hail and rain, combined with a cloud base of 1,000 feet and a strong wind – had prevented any operations taking place. The crews had even been given a couple of days leave to enjoy the local area before the weather finally improved enough for the two Whitleys to conduct the drop on Warsaw.

At 7.20 p.m. on the evening of 15 March, Tomlin eased back on the controls to lift the Whitley, N1387 KN-L 'Love', into the sky. Having been given a course to fly by his observer, Sergeant Ron Charlton, he headed for the Polish capital. Twenty minutes behind him, and with the same task, was the second Whitley flown by Flying Officer Gordon Raphael. Even by operating

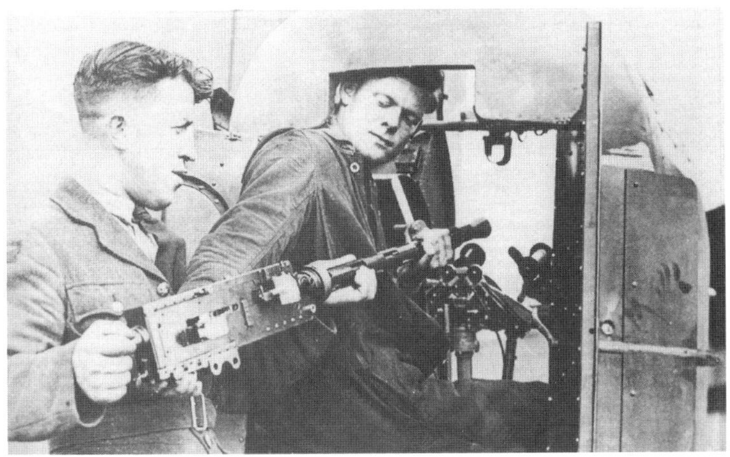

Armourers servicing a Whitley. (via Ken Delve)

from an airfield in north-east France, the Whitley's slow speed in difficult weather conditions made it a long transit but, eventually, the aircraft arrived overhead Warsaw. Having dropped their Nickels, Tomlin headed back across Germany without incident, although the weather conditions made navigation difficult and fuel was starting to get low. Finally, convinced they had returned back across the Franco–German frontier, Tomlin put the aircraft down in a large field, a near text book landing.

Unbeknown to the crew they had landed in Germany some fifteen miles behind enemy lines. It was only after the crew had vacated the aircraft and spoke with a local that it became obvious they had landed in Germany. German troops were now approaching and so the crew quickly dashed back to the aircraft and jumped on board. Tomlin turned into wind and pushed the throttles forward as quickly as he could. The Whitley limped into the air under enemy fire and soon landed safely back in France, at an airfield at Nancy, albeit with its crew rather shaken after their ordeal. They had landed back in France at 4.15 a.m., some nine hours after they had first taken off. Raphael, meanwhile, had landed safely at a French airfield at Villeneuve having been airborne for more than eleven hours.

The Whitley crews were now used to being away from their home base. There were not only the short detachments to France for Nickelling but the Whitley also proved versatile enough for the crews to be detached away from Driffield to work with Coastal Command.

A rather unusual occurrence saw 97 Squadron re-formed at Driffield on 1 May only to disband again on the 20th without having received any aircraft. It would be another year before this bomber squadron would re-form properly but this was not the only occasion when a squadron number plate was associated with Driffield for a matter of days. The following month the surviving Fairey Battles of 88 Squadron arrived in Yorkshire, having suffered heavily during the fall of France, only to leave a week later for Northern Ireland where the squadron could fully recover before moving to Norfolk to resume operations over Europe.

With Italy entering the war the following month, Driffield's Whitleys were involved in the first raid against an Italian target on the night of 11/12 June 1940. Thirty-six aircraft first flew to the Channel Islands to refuel before carrying out their long flight over the Alps to bomb factories in Turin. Because of the difficult weather encountered over the Alps, including thunderstorms and severe icing, only nine aircraft reached Turin. One aircraft of 77 Squadron, flown by Sergeant Norman Songest, crashed near Le Mans on the return flight, killing all on board. These were Bomber Command's first casualties in the war on Italy.

With the Battle of Britain raging over southern England, Driffield's Whitley squadrons continued to take the war to Nazi Germany whenever they could. So important was Driffield considered to be by German intelligence that it was attacked by the Luftwaffe during the afternoon of 15 August. Instead of heading for RAF airfields in the south-east of England, a small force of Ju 88s crossed the North Sea from their base in Denmark to attack Driffield. More than 150 bombs fell on the airfield, causing considerable damage to four hangars and many other buildings. Twelve Whitleys were destroyed on the ground and fourteen of the station's personnel were killed, with many more left wounded.

The Luftwaffe's attack on Driffield had been so destructive that it put the airfield out of action for the rest of the year. It later proved to be the Luftwaffe's most devastating attack against an RAF bomber airfield of the war. What was left of the two

Whitley squadrons was forced to move out; 102 Squadron to Leeming and 77 to Linton-on-Ouse. In an attempt to prevent a repeat, decoy sites were built at Kilham and Skerne, complete with dummy aircraft. Dummy Whitley bombers were also placed at Driffield to give German intelligence the impression that the airfield was still operational and to hide the fact that the squadrons had been forced to move out.

Driffield opened again in January 1941 but not as a bomber airfield. For the next three months it was allocated to Fighter Command and home to Hurricanes and Spitfires before Driffield was transferred back to Bomber Command and to 4 Group. In April, 104 Squadron re-formed with Wellingtons and Driffield was to be the squadron's home for the next ten months. Within days, another Wellington squadron had formed at Driffield. This was 405 (Vancouver) Squadron RCAF, the first Canadian bomber squadron to be formed overseas.

Bomber operations resumed from Driffield on the night of 8/9 May 1941 when six of 104's aircraft joined fifty more Wellingtons and nearly eighty Whitleys in an attack against the German port of Bremen. The following month 405 flew its, and the RCAF's, first bombing operation of the war when four of its Wellingtons joined eighty Whitleys to attack railway yards at Schwerte near Dortmund. Unfortunately, the target was covered by haze, making it difficult for the crews to bomb. Although three Whitleys were lost during the night, all four of 405's Wellingtons returned.

A week later, 405 Squadron moved out, leaving 104 as Driffield's only resident squadron, although a handful of Whitleys of 2 Beam Approach Training Flight had moved in; this unit was later re-designated 1502 BATF. During this period, Driffield was also home to various types of aircraft serving with 4 Group's Target Towing Flight (later re-numbered 1484 Target Towing Flight), including more Whitleys, Lysanders and Battles.

By now, 104 Squadron had been split. Half the squadron remained at Driffield while the other half detached to Malta, but early in 1942 the squadron's move to Malta became permanent. Its home cadre stayed behind to form 158 Squadron with Wellington IIs and the new squadron flew its first operations in February against Mannheim, although the squadron would re-equip with Halifaxes in June.

At this stage of the war, Driffield was still an all-grass airfield and it was now time for it to undergo further reconstruction. Over the next few months, aircraft and squadrons came and went. First, 158 Squadron left for East Moor in June but unfortunately the squadron departed on a sad note. Its last operational mission from Driffield had been against Cologne on what was the first of the Thousand Bomber raids. Two of the squadron's aircraft had failed to return, including Z8577 'NP-T' flown by 25-year-old Squadron Leader Don Harkness DFC from New Zealand, who had led the squadron that night. His Wellington had taken off from Driffield just after 11 p.m. but because of heavy icing encountered on the way to the target Harkness had been unable to climb to the required transit height. Nonetheless, he refused to turn back and pressed on below 10,000 feet but the Wellington was picked up by searchlights as it crossed the Dutch coast and was then pounced on by a German night fighter. The Wellington came down in the eastern Scheldt with the loss of all on board. It appears the second of the squadron's Wellingtons lost that night, flown by Pilot Officer Ralph O'Brien, a 24-year-old Canadian, suffered a similar fate.

466 (RAAF) Squadron and 196 Squadron both formed at Driffield with Wellingtons during October and November but by the end of 1942 both squadrons had left for Leconfield so that construction work could take place. Driffield was again non-operational as the airfield was brought up to standard with three concrete runways (the main, 2,000 yards long, ran from the north-east to the south-west), a perimeter track, hard standings for thirty-six aircraft, five hangars for maintenance and enough accommodation for nearly 2,500 personnel.

Under the RAF's re-organization in early 1943, Driffield became Headquarters 43 Base with its sub-stations at Leconfield and Lissett. Although still temporarily closed to flying, many ground personnel passed through Driffield to attend various training courses that were still being run on the station.

It was not until June 1944 that Driffield became fully active again when the Australians of 466 Squadron, now equipped with four-engine Halifaxes, returned from Leconfield under the command of Wing Commander H W Connolly. It was just hours until D-Day and during the days that followed Driffield's

Halifaxes supported the Allied landings in Normandy and the subsequent breakout towards Germany.

In August, a second Australian Halifax squadron moved in. This was 462 (RAAF) Squadron under the command of Wing Commander David Shannon DFC, which re-formed at Driffield after returning from the campaign in Italy. However, this second Aussie squadron's stay in Yorkshire was short-lived, although it did fly on nearly forty operations from Driffield, as by the end of the year 462 had been transferred to 100 (Bomber Support) Group for Special Duties as a radio countermeasures squadron.

In October command of 466 Squadron passed to Wing Commander A Wharton. Driffield saw out the last months of the war with 466 as its only operational residents. One lucky member of the squadron was Flying Officer Joe Herman, an experienced Australian pilot. Herman was the captain of a Halifax taking part in a raid against Bochum on the night of 4/5 November 1944. Having been hit by flak he ordered his crew to bale out but before he could make his own escape he noticed one of his crew, the mid-upper gunner, Flight Sergeant 'Irish' Vivash, was trapped. As Herman tried to rescue his gunner the aircraft fell apart, causing him to fall without his parachute. Remarkably, he escaped with his life having grabbed Vivash, who had also been blown clear of the aircraft, with both men coming down on one parachute, albeit rather heavily, to become prisoners of war.

Like other bomber airfields in eastern England, Driffield received an unwelcome visitor on the night of 3/4 March 1945. The raider was a Ju 88G, which was part of a large intruder force under the Luftwaffe's Operation *Gisela*. It was effectively the Luftwaffe's last roll of the dice and was designed to take Bomber Command and the British defences by surprise. In some ways Gisela worked. Many Ju 88s crossed the North Sea to create havoc amongst Bomber Command's aircraft returning from operations over Germany, including Halifaxes from 4 Group returning to Yorkshire following a raid against a synthetic oil refinery at Bergkamen. Amongst the many RAF bomber crews to have been taken by surprise that night were two Halifax crews returning to Driffield. Both Halifaxes were in the airfield's circuit and about to land when they were attacked. One of the crews managed to bale out and survived, but the second crew were not so lucky. Their Halifax crashed near the airfield with four of the crew killed.

The last bombing operation of the war from Driffield was flown on 25 April 1945 when eighteen of 466's Halifaxes took part in the raid against the coastal batteries on the Frisian island of Wangerooge. With hostilities over, Driffield was briefly transferred to Transport Command but when the airfield was placed on care and maintenance before the end of the year, its future looked uncertain. Fortunately, though, it was retained in the post-war RAF and passed to Flying Training Command. However, the role of the station would change yet again during the mid-1950s when it was transferred to Fighter Command. But even this change was short-lived, as Driffield was chosen to be the headquarters for a Thor missile complex with satellites at Breighton, Carnaby, Catfoss and Full Sutton, taking the airfield full circle back into Bomber Command.

At the end of the Thor era in 1963, Driffield closed once again. However, its flying days were not yet over as Driffield continued to be used until 1977, including the test flying of Buccaneer aircraft being built at Brough. The airfield was then transferred

Driffield's two Australian squadrons are remembered in the Memorial Gardens in the town. Their memorial stands between the District of Driffield Memorial (on the left of photo) and a memorial to the fourteen station personnel killed during the air raid of 15 August 1940, which has recently been relocated having once stood outside the station headquarters. (Author)

to the army to become Alamein Barracks. It was another case of the airfield having passed full circle back to where its life had first begun.

The former airfield can be found two miles south-west of the market town of Driffield between the A614 that runs south-west towards Market Weighton and the A166 to York. Following the A614 from Driffield first takes you south to a roundabout at Kelleythorpe, after which the road runs in a more westerly direction. The former airfield is on your right with the village of Eastburn marking its western boundary. The entrance to the airfield, where the administrative site was situated, as were the hangars, is all off to your right, although there were also some aircraft dispersals to your left on the southern side of the main road.

A memorial to Driffield's two Australian squadrons – 462 and 466 (RAAF) Squadrons – can be found in the Memorial Gardens in the town, as can the District of Driffield Memorial dedicated to its locals killed during the Second World War. There is also a memorial to the fourteen station personnel killed during the air raid of 15 August 1940, which has been relocated in recent years having once stood outside the station headquarters. The Memorial Gardens can be found on the corner of North Street and East Gate North.

Summary of units based at Driffield during the Second World War

102 Squadron (DY) – Jul 38 (Honington) – 24 Aug 40 (Leeming)
Whitley III/V

77 Squadron (KN) – Jul 38 (Honington) – 27 Aug 40 (Linton-on-Ouse)
Whitley III/V

97 Squadron – 1 – 20 May 40
No aircraft

88 Squadron (RH) – 14 – 22 Jun 40
Battle

104 Squadron (EP) – 1 Apr 41 (Re-formed) – 13 Feb 42 (Malta)
Wellington II

405 Squadron RCAF (LQ) – 23 Apr 41 (Formed) – 19 Jun 41 (Pocklington)
Wellington II

158 Squadron (NP) – 14 Feb 42 (Formed) – 5 Jun 42 (East Moor)
Wellington II (Feb – Jun 42)
Halifax II (Jun 42)

466 (RAAF) Squadron (HD) – 15 Oct 42 (Formed) – 26 Dec 42 (Leconfield)
Wellington III

196 Squadron (ZO) – 7 Nov 42 (Formed) – 21 Dec 42 (Leconfield)
Wellington X

466 (RAAF) Squadron (HD) – 3 Jun 44 (Leconfield) – 7 Sep 45 (Bassingbourn)
Halifax III

462 (RAAF) Squadron (Z5) – 12 Aug 44 (Re-formed) – 28 Dec 44 (Foulsham)
Halifax III

Chapter 7

Elvington

Location – North Yorkshire, seven miles south-east of York.
Status – Satellite airfield. 42 Base – sub-station of Pocklington.

Now home to the Yorkshire Air Museum, this former wartime bomber airfield dates back to the early years of the Second World War. Built on Langwith Common, work initially began in 1940 to construct a grass airfield for Bomber Command, but with heavier bombers already in the pipeline the plan for the site had to be reviewed. The limitations of the heathland on which the airfield was built, and its position

A Halifax of 77 Squadron coming in to land at Elvington. (Tom Treadwell via Ken Delve)

between two large woods, required a complete rethink for Elvington and so it was not until two years later that work was complete.

Elvington finally opened in October 1942, and allocated to 4 Group as a satellite of Pocklington. It had been constructed with three hardened runways with the main, 2,000 yards long, running east-west. A single intersection and a perimeter track connected the runways, three maintenance hangars were built on loops at the south-east corner of the airfield, along with technical and domestic buildings, and there was enough accommodation for more than 2,500 personnel on the eastern part of the site.

The first aircraft to operate from Elvington were Whitleys of 77 Squadron, which immediately moved to Yorkshire from Devon having been detached to Coastal Command for the past six months. The Whitleys were soon replaced by Halifaxes in time for 77 Squadron to commence operations in early 1943.

The squadron was then under the command of Wing Commander John Embling, a pre-war flight cadet with the Oxford University Air Squadron and then a graduate entrant at the RAF College Cranwell. Embling had taken over command of 77 from Donald Bennett, now leading the Pathfinders, and would go on to survive the war to enjoy a long and successful post-war career in the RAF, but his life could so easily have ended soon after he took command of 77. While the squadron was working up to operational standard with the Halifax, some of its pilots flew on ops with 102 Squadron at Pocklington. Embling was one of those to take the opportunity to gain some early operational experience with the Halifax and so he flew as second pilot to 23-year-old Squadron Leader John Walkington, one of 102's flight commanders, on the Frankfurt raid on the night of 2/3 December 1942. With just over a hundred aircraft involved, the raid was not a particularly large one, but while over France their Halifax was jumped by an enemy night fighter and shot down. Walkington was one of three members of the crew to die, while Embling and the others managed to bale out; two of which, including Embling, managed to evade capture and eventually made it back to England.

By the time Embling returned home, command of the squadron had passed to Wing Commander Arthur Lowe, known to his men as 'Lofty' and the first air gunner to command a bomber squadron. Lowe had joined the RAF in the early 1930s at the age of sixteen, and first trained as a wireless mechanic before he volunteered to train as an air gunner. By the outbreak of war, he was serving with 77 Squadron as a Whitley gunner. In early 1940, he was commissioned and he had then worked his way up to acting wing commander and was now in command of the same squadron.

Lowe oversaw his squadron's work up with the Halifax to the point of operational readiness. The squadron's first op with the type was flown on the night of 4/5 February 1943. It was a night when Bomber Command split its resources between a raid on Turin and the U-boat pens in the French Atlantic port of Lorient, with 77 Squadron involved in the latter.

By the time the squadron became immersed in the hard-fought Battle of Berlin during the winter of 1943/44, command of 77 had passed to Wing Commander John Roncoroni, who had taken over from Lofty Lowe in October 1943. The squadron remained at Elvington until May 1944, by which time its Halifax IIs had been exchanged for Mark Vs. In just over a year of operations from Elvington, the squadron had lost more than eighty aircraft, with the loss of some 450 lives.

Elvington's next residents were not to be British or Canadian, like many of Yorkshire's bomber airfields, but French. Two new Halifax squadrons formed at Elvington during 1944 and both

A Halifax VI of 346 (Guyenne) Squadron, one of two French heavy bomber squadrons formed at Elvington in 1944. (via Ken Delve)

would remain for the rest of the war. The first to form was 346 (Guyenne) Squadron under the command of Lieutenant Colonel Gaston Venot. Made up of French personnel who had arrived in England from service in North Africa, the squadron commenced operations on the night of 1/2 June 1944 when a dozen of its aircraft took part in an all-Halifax raid against a German radio listening station at Ferme-d'Urville. The raid was one of a number along the northern coastline of France, all intended to soften up German defences in preparation for D-Day, now just a few days away. All of 346's aircraft returned safely.

Later in the month the second French bomber squadron formed at Elvington. This was 347 (Tunise) Squadron, also made up of French personnel returning from North Africa, which commenced operations almost immediately. On the night of 27/28 June it contributed a dozen Halifaxes to a large force of 700-plus aircraft tasked with carrying out attacks against six V-1 weapon sites in northern France.

The Halifax was a versatile aircraft and in late September the two Elvington squadrons were tasked with ferrying thousands of gallons of fuel to Belgium to support the British Second Army as it made its advance towards Germany. In one week the two squadrons each flew more than a hundred sorties and between them delivered nearly 200,000 gallons of petrol.

With their temporary transport duties over the two French squadrons returned to their more familiar role of bombing. Elvington was now fully established with Free French personnel and under the command of an officer of the French Air Force.

Although the war was in its final phase, Elvington was one of a number of Yorkshire airfields to receive an unwelcome visitor on the night of 3/4 March 1945. It was the night the Luftwaffe launched Operation *Gisela*, a mass intruder raid by Ju 88s over eastern England, which took Bomber Command and the British defences completely by surprise. The Elvington crews were returning from an attack against a synthetic oil refinery at Bergkamen when word of the Luftwaffe intruders spread. In all, twenty RAF bombers were shot down over English soil that night, including three from Elvington, and another dozen or more badly damaged. More than eighty men were dead and many more injured. Several targets of opportunity, such as airfields and railway yards, had also been attacked. Three of the

German intruders were lost over eastern England having hit the ground while flying too low in the dark. The third of these came down after hitting some trees while attacking a Halifax coming in to land at Elvington. It was the last Luftwaffe aircraft of the war to come down on English soil, with the loss of all its crew.

Elvington's two French bomber squadrons flew their last operations on 25 April 1945 when thirty aircraft joined a 4 Group raid against gun batteries on the Frisian island of Wangerooge. The raid involved more than 300 Halifaxes with five failing to return, including one belonging to 347 Squadron.

During their year at Elvington the two French squadrons had flown well over 2,500 sorties for the loss of thirty aircraft. With the war over both squadrons ceased to be part of the RAF and returned to France, taking with them their Halifaxes. Elvington had been their only home. The airfield was then transferred to Maintenance Command but Elvington did have a new lease of life during the 1950s when it was used by the Americans. Millions of dollars were pumped into improving the airfield and its facilities, which included extending the runway and the construction of new buildings, but a change in foreign policy saw the Americans leave almost as quickly as they had arrived

Elvington is now home to the Yorkshire Air Museum. The original control tower and many of the airfield's wartime buildings still stand and give a marvellous insight into what this former wartime bomber airfield was once like. (Author)

and by the end of the decade they had gone. During the 1960s Elvington was used as a relief landing ground for Church Fenton and then, during the 1970s, for Leeming and Linton-on-Ouse, after which the airfield was declared surplus to requirement. RAF Elvington closed in 1992 and was sold by the Ministry of Defence in 1999.

While the main runway survived for private flying, and was also used over the years for motor sport, it is thanks to the vision of a local resident that the history of this former wartime bomber airfield has been preserved as the Yorkshire Air Museum, which is run today by a dedicated team of volunteers. The museum can be found on the western side of Elvington, off the B1228 Elvington Lane by taking the appropriately named Halifax Way, which leads down to the airfield industrial park, and then Whitley Road to the right. Amongst the many original buildings that have survived is the air traffic control tower. A new hangar accommodates a wonderful collection of historic aircraft, including the restored version of the RAF's most famous Halifax *Friday the Thirteenth*. It is a hybrid airframe rebuilt from a fuselage section of a Halifax II (HR792) and the wings of a Handley Page Hastings, and put together by enthusiasts using a number of parts of Halifax aircraft recovered from all round

The Memorial Garden at the Yorkshire Air Museum. In addition to being an aviation museum, Elvington is also the Allied Air Forces Memorial, a fundamental reason for the founding of the museum. (Author)

The memorial to the two French wartime squadrons that operated from the airfield can be found on Elvington Lane. (Author)

the world. While one side of the aircraft carries the markings of *Friday The Thirteenth,* the other is painted in the scheme of a Free French variant 'N-November'. It proudly represents the 6,176 Halifax bombers built during the Second World War and is testament to the efforts of those who flew and maintained them during the aircraft's short and decisive history. There is so much to see at the museum. For example, a Memorial Garden includes memorials to Yorkshire's two bomber groups – 4 Group and 6 (RCAF) Group – and another is to the men and women of the Air Transport Auxiliary. The Yorkshire Air Museum relies on funding from its small entrance charge and donations but it is a must visit for all historians and aviation enthusiasts.

In the village of Elvington there is a memorial to the two French wartime bomber squadrons that operated from the airfield; it can be found on Elvington Lane by turning right on leaving the museum.

Summary of units based at Elvington during the Second World War

77 Squadron (KN) – 5 Oct 42 (Chivenor) – 14 May 44 (Full Sutton)
Halifax II (Oct 42 – May 44)
Halifax V (Apr – May 44)

346 (Guyenne) Squadron (H7) – 16 May 44 (Formed) – 20 Oct 45 (Disbanded)
Halifax V (May – Jun 44)
Halifax III (Jun 44 – Apr 45)
Halifax VI (Mar – Oct 45)

347 (Tunise) Squadron (L8) – 20 Jun 44 (Formed) – 20 Oct 45 (Disbanded)
Halifax V (May – Jun 44)
Halifax III (Jun 44 – Apr 45)
Halifax VI (Mar – Oct 45)

CHAPTER 8

Full Sutton

Location – East Riding of Yorkshire, nine miles east of York.
Status – Satellite airfield. 42 Base – sub-station of Pocklington.

The last bomber airfield to become operational in Yorkshire was Full Sutton. Although its wartime operational existence was less than a year the airfield was, nonetheless, very active and its only residents, 77 Squadron, were involved in most of Bomber Command's major efforts during the latter months of the war.

Allocated to 4 Group, the airfield opened in May 1944. Built on common land, it had been completed to the standard bomber airfield design with three concrete runways. The longest was 2,000 yards in length and was aligned just off north-south, while two shorter subsidiaries, 1,600 yards and 1,400 yards respectively, were linked by a perimeter track. Thirty-six aircraft dispersals were constructed in half a dozen loops around the track, and there was enough domestic accommodation for nearly 2,000 personnel.

Having not opened until the final year of the war, only one operational squadron was ever to be based at Full Sutton. This was 77 Squadron, and when it first arrived it was in the process of taking delivery of Halifax IIIs to replace its Mark IIs and Mark Vs. The squadron flew its first operation from Full Sutton on the night of 1/2 June 1944 at a time when Bomber Command was softening up German defences along the northern coastline of France. The target was the German's main radio listening station at Ferme-d'Urville. No aircraft were lost but poor weather prevented accurate bombing and so the target had to be re-visited two nights later; this time by Lancasters of 5 Group.

A Halifax of 77 Squadron during its take-off run. Full Sutton was the last bomber airfield to become operational in Yorkshire and 77 was its only resident squadron. (AHB)

Full Sutton may well have been a latecomer to the war, but it did not escape heavy losses. An example was the night of 16/17 June, which was to prove 77 Squadron's worst night of the war when it took part in a raid against a synthetic oil plant at Sterkrade in the industrial Ruhr. The total force taking part in the raid was over 300 aircraft, half of which were Halifaxes of which 77 Squadron contributed twenty-three. The route to the target took the force through an area of intense night fighter activity. Anti-aircraft flak also proved accurate and the overall result was the loss of thirty-one bombers, two-thirds of which were Halifaxes. This put the overall loss rate for the type at nearly 14 per cent. Seven of the Halifaxes lost belonged to 77 Squadron, nearly one-third of those that had set off from Full Sutton.

The losses that night were felt by all at Full Sutton but life had to go on. The fact that the Allies were now firmly back in north-west Europe and advancing towards Germany would no doubt have buoyed everyone on. Replacements arrived and soon the squadron was nearly back to full strength.

Being a Halifax squadron, the crews found themselves involved in the massive air lift of fuel during September and

October 1944 to re-supply the British Second Army in Belgium, after which normal bombing operations were resumed. During the latter weeks of the war the squadron converted to the Halifax VI and flew its last operations of the war against the gun batteries on the Frisian island of Wangerooge. With hostilities over, the squadron was transferred to Transport Command. During its time at Full Sutton, it had lost nearly thirty aircraft.

Full Sutton was not part of the RAF's post-war plans but the airfield did survive for many years. After 77 Squadron moved out in August 1945, a number of transport units came and went until two years later, when the airfield was placed on care and maintenance. Not much happened for the next few years until Full Sutton re-opened during the early-1950s as a training school during the period of the Korean War. From the mid-50s, the airfield was designated as a reserve site for the American Strategic Air Command but just two years later the airfield was returned to the RAF, after which it was home to a Thor missile squadron until 1963 when Full Sutton finally closed.

Since then the land has been used for a variety of purposes. The air traffic control tower was demolished in 2003 and the former technical site was redeveloped as a farm and industrial estate, which was built up around the original area of the perimeter track. Part of the site was also redeveloped to become HMP Full

Full Sutton has retained its link with its flying past as part of the former wartime airfield is still used by the Full Sutton Flying Centre. (Author)

Sutton, one of the country's highest security prisons. However, Full Sutton has retained its link with the past as part of the former airfield is still used by the Full Sutton Flying Centre. A grass strip running from the north-east to the south-west marks the line of one of the original wartime runways and is currently used for light aircraft flying.

When travelling eastwards along the A166 from Stamford Bridge towards Driffield, the airfield can be found by taking a right turn towards the village of Full Sutton. Continue southwards along that minor road and at the T-junction of Moor Lane turn left (turning right takes you towards the prison); this marks the northern extremity of the former airfield. Turn left into Moor Lane, which soon becomes Hatkill Lane, and this takes you southwards along the eastern boundary of the former airfield. After about half a mile, turn right into Common Lane and this takes you into an industrial estate. You will then need to weave your way through the industrial estate, first to the right and then to the left (there are some signs to the Flying Centre to help). You will, however, need to park short of reaching the Flying Centre (unless you have prior permission to proceed) as part of what was the airfield's main runway is still used by aircraft. You will then see the buildings of the Full Sutton Flying Centre to your right.

Summary of units based at Full Sutton during the Second World War

77 Squadron (KN) – 15 May 44 (Elvington) – 30 Aug 45 (Broadwell)
Halifax III (May 44 – Mar 45)
Halifax VI (Mar – Aug 45)

Chapter 9

Holme-on-Spalding Moor

Location – East Riding of Yorkshire, four miles south-west of Market Weighton.
Status – Operational airfield. HQ 44 Base.

Another Yorkshire airfield developed for Bomber Command during the Second World War was Holme-on-Spalding Moor. Developed on Holme Common, a flat area of land just above sea-level, the airfield was built during the early months of the war and first opened in the summer of 1941. The combination of the drainage dykes and local roads had determined the layout of the airfield and so it ended up with a rather unusual kink along the northern part of the perimeter track, where the administrative site was built and where the control tower was located. Otherwise, the runways were tarmac with the main, 1,800 yards long, running from the south-east corner of the airfield to the north-west. The two subsidiaries were each around 1,200 yards long and linked by the perimeter track, off which thirty-six aircraft hard standings were constructed around the site.

Being close to the Humber estuary meant that Holme was close to the bomber airfields of 1 Group in northern Lincolnshire and so it was to 1 Group, rather than 4 Group, that Holme-on-Spalding Moor was initially allocated. The first aircraft to arrive were twin-engine Airspeed Oxfords of 20 Beam Approach Training Flight, later re-designated 1520 BATF. The first bombers to arrive at Holme were Wellingtons of the newly formed 458 (RAAF) Squadron. This squadron had formed in New South Wales in Australia under the Empire Air Training Scheme.

Preparing for the night's op. Ground personnel and a Halifax of 76 Squadron at Holme-on-Spalding Moor. (via Ken Delve)

Destined for operations in Europe, its ground echelon had made the long journey from Australia by sea.

By the night of 20/21 October 1941, the squadron was ready to commence its first bombing operation. It was a night when Bomber Command split its resources. The squadron had prepared ten Wellingtons for ops that night and so eight joined a small force of thirty-five aircraft going to Antwerp, while two joined a similar sized force going to Emden. One squadron aircraft from the Antwerp raid failed to return with the loss of five of the crew.

Under its first commanding officer, Wing Commander Norman Mulholland, an experienced bomber pilot with a DFC from his previous tour, the squadron took part in many of Bomber Command's major raids against Germany before it received notification of a move to the Middle East. The squadron flew its last operations from Holme against Boulogne docks on the night of 28/29 January 1942, after which it began preparing for its move overseas.

For a while, Holme was used by a number of non-operational aircraft as the airfield underwent further reconstruction. Many lessons had been learned from its first brief experience of operating Wellingtons and so several improvements were put in place, such as the construction of new maintenance hangars, of which six were eventually built, in preparation for the arrival of the four-engine Halifax. However, although efforts were made to improve the domestic facilities on base, they were never considered to be great by many of those who served there.

The first aircraft to use the airfield after its makeover were from 460 (RAAF) Squadron based at Breighton. It was the summer of 1942 and the Australians were in the process of converting from the Wellington to the Halifax, and so the squadron's conversion flight used Holme-on-Spalding Moor as an overflow from its home base, although 460 Squadron never made Holme its home.

The first resident unit to move in to the new Holme-on-Spalding Moor was 1503 Beam Approach Training Flight. This training unit would leave at the turn of the year to be replaced by Oxfords of 1520 BATF, which, in turn, would move out just a few months later. But in September 1942, Holme became home to an operational squadron once again. This was 101 Squadron, a squadron that had previously served at Stradishall in the all-Wellington 3 Group but was now converting to the Lancaster to become the first 1 Group squadron to be so equipped, and so it was only a matter of weeks before the last of the squadron's Wellingtons had left.

Holme-on-Spalding Moor witnessed a tragic incident on the night of 23/24 October 1942 when a Halifax of 102 Squadron based at Pocklington diverted to Holme after returning from a raid on Genoa. The aircraft was flown by the squadron commander, 29-year-old Wing Commander Bruce Bintley, but had been unable to land at its own airfield because of bad weather. It had already been a long night for Bintley and his crew and it was around 3.30 a.m. when the aircraft, DT512 'DY-Q', touched down at Holme in poor visibility. But as it did so, one of its front tyres burst. The Halifax swung off the runway and came to rest with its front end sticking out over the active runway. Just a minute later a second Halifax, 'DY-D' flown by Flight Sergeant Eddie Berry, came in to land. Bintley's Halifax was still stationary where it had come to rest and there had been no time to clear it from danger. There was nothing that could be done. The second Halifax came down on the first, taking out the forward fuselage and killing two of the crew, including Bintley. The second crew member to be killed was Flight Lieutenant

Arthur Graham, a 23-year-old air gunner from Canada. The rest of the crew, and that of the second aircraft, escaped with their lives. Wing Commander Sydney Bruce Bintley DSO AFC, from Reigate in Surrey, and Arthur Graham from Montreal, are both buried in Barmby-on-the-Moor (St Catherine) churchyard.

101 Squadron started 1943 under the command of its popular CO, Wing Commander D A Reddick. As a pre-war sergeant pilot with the squadron, Reddick had thrilled crowds at Hendon in 1936 when he looped, rolled and stall-turned a twin-engine Boulton Paul Overstrand medium bomber while in mock combat manoeuvres with Hawker Fury fighters. Reddick was to now lead 101 Squadron through the hard-fought Battle of the Ruhr.

During a raid against Dortmund on the night of 4/5 May 1943, six of 101's aircraft were lost. The raid involved nearly 600 aircraft, making it the largest since the Thousand Bomber raids a year before, and it was the first attack against this industrial target. But the result was mixed. Many bombs fell outside the designated target and a total of thirty-one aircraft were lost, including the six Lancasters from Holme-on-Spalding Moor.

At that time Holme was under the command of Group Captain Robert Blucke, a former First World War army officer, who was awarded the DSO while flying with the squadron during a raid against Mannheim. Despite his aircraft being hit and badly damaged during his bombing run, Blucke had managed to complete the attack and then get his badly damaged Lancaster back home.

Following a change in Bomber Command's group boundaries, and with 101 being a Lancaster squadron, the squadron and Blucke moved to Ludford Magna in Lincolnshire in June 1943, where it would remain for the rest of the war. Command of Holme-on-Spalding Moor now passed to an Australian, Group Captain D E L Wilson, with the airfield transferring to 4 Group as Headquarters 44 Base.

Two days after the last of 101 Squadron had left, the first Halifaxes of 76 Squadron started moving in from Linton-on-Ouse. Holme would be its home for the rest of the war and the new arrivals commenced operations almost immediately, taking part in an attack against Le Creusot on the night of 19/20 June. The target was the French equivalent to the Krupps armaments factories in the Ruhr and one of Bomber Command's highest priority targets.

Three nights later, the target was the German town of Mülheim but one aircraft failed to return, that with the base commander on board. Wilson's Halifax had been shot down by a night fighter but he had managed to bale out to be taken as a prisoner of war. With the loss of Wilson, command of the base was given to Group Captain G S Hodson.

The rest of 1943 proved to be particularly hard for the Halifax squadrons, including 76. Amongst Bomber Command's losses during this period were forty aircraft from Holme-on-Spalding Moor. 76 Squadron was now under the command of 26-year-old Wing Commander Hank Iveson, a local from the East Riding, who took over command at the end of the year. He had already earned the DFC during his previous tour with the squadron the year before while based at Middleton St George. While commanding 76 Squadron, Iveson would add a Bar to his DFC and the DSO, and would later enjoy a successful post-war career in the RAF.

In early 1944, 76 Squadron exchanged its Halifax Vs for improved Mark IIIs. By the end of the war, the squadron would be operating the Halifax VI, which all helped bring the squadron's loss rate down during the latter months of the war, although this is not entirely attributable to the change of aircraft marks. It was a period when Bomber Command's overall loss rate was reducing due to the Luftwaffe's night fighter force becoming stretched across all fronts, and also because of its shortage of fuel.

Holme-on-Spalding Moor had also welcomed the Spitfires, Hurricanes and Martinets of 1689 Bomber Defence Training Flight, which had replaced 1520 BATF as a fighter affiliation unit for the bomber crews of 4 Group. During the last year of the war Holme was commanded by Group Captain J E Pelly-Fry. Like other Halifax squadrons, 76's last operations of the war were flown on 25 April 1945 against gun batteries on the Frisian island of Wangerooge. Twenty-five of the squadron's aircraft took part in the raid, although two failed to return.

76 Squadron had flown more operational sorties than any other Halifax squadron, but it had lost more than a hundred aircraft during its time at Holme-on-Spalding Moor. With hostilities

Much of Holme-on-Spalding Moor has long reverted to its pre-war agricultural use. This is the south-east corner of the former airfield, where Skiff Lane meets Drain Lane, marking where the threshold of the main runway was. (Author)

over, the BDTF moved out and the airfield was transferred to Transport Command, with 76 Squadron converting to the Dakota before moving out to prepare for a move overseas. It was replaced by another Dakota squadron, although within weeks this squadron had also left for overseas.

With all flying units gone, Holme-on-Spalding Moor was placed on care and maintenance. Like some of Yorkshire's other bomber airfields, Holme was retained and had a new lease of life during the Korean War of the early 1950s when it was used as a training base. The airfield was then briefly used by the Americans, during which time the main runway was extended, before Holme-on-Spalding Moor was taken over by Blackburn Aviation in 1958 as a satellite for its main factory at nearby Brough where the runway was not long enough for the testing of its new aircraft, the Buccaneer. For more than twenty years, Holme-on-Spalding Moor was used in this capacity, although company changes saw the airfield later come under the auspices of Hawker Siddeley and then British Aerospace until the latter ceased using the airfield in 1983.

Much of the land has since reverted to its pre-war agricultural use, although part of the former airfield is now an industrial estate. The runways and perimeter track have long gone but many of the airfield's former technical buildings still stand, including two old hangars.

The site of the former airfield can be found by taking the A614 Howden Road south from the village of Holme-on-Spalding Moor. At the end of the village is a turning left called Port Royal. Follow this and after less than 100 yards the road bears right into Skiff Lane. Follow the lane for just over a mile and on your right is an industrial estate, built on what was the former administrative and technical sites. If you turn into the estate, you will see on your left a memorial to 76 Squadron and a memorial plaque and tree to 458 (RAAF) Squadron, standing on what was the main entrance to the airfield. Behind the memorial are other plaques in memory of some of those who served at the airfield during the war, including Group Captain Hank Iveson DSO DFC and Bar, who commanded 76 Squadron at Holme during 1943/44, and to Lord Cheshire VC OM DSO DFC who had commanded the squadron earlier in the war. If you continue past the industrial estate along the narrowing Skiff Lane you come to the eastern end of the former airfield. The lane continues south and then westwards onto Drain Lane along the former airfield's southern boundary. This road will eventually take you back to the A614 Howden Road.

An industrial estate has been built on what was the administrative and technical sites of Holme. A memorial to 76 Squadron and a memorial plaque and tree to 458 (RAAF) Squadron stand on what was the main entrance to the airfield. (Author)

Summary of units based at Holme-on-Spalding Moor during the Second World War

458 (RAAF) Squadron (FU) – 25 Aug 41 (Formed) – 20 Mar 42 (Middle East)
Wellington IV

101 Squadron (SR) – 29 Sep 42 (Stradishall) – 14 Jun 43 (Ludford Magna)
Wellington III (Sep – Oct 42)
Lancaster I (Oct 42 – Jun 43)

76 Squadron (SR) – 16 Jun 43 (Linton-on-Ouse) – 5 Aug 45 (Broadwell)
Halifax V (Jun 43 – Feb 44)
Halifax III (Feb 44 – Apr 45)
Halifax VI (Mar – Aug 45)

Chapter 10

Leconfield

Location – East Riding of Yorkshire, two miles north of Beverley.
Status – Operational airfield. 43 Base – sub-station of Driffield.

Built as part of the RAF's Expansion Scheme of the mid-1930s, Leconfield opened as a bomber airfield in 1936. Initially allocated to 3 Group, the airfield was soon transferred to 4 Group as part of Bomber Command's re-organization and by the outbreak of the Second World War was home to two squadrons of Whitleys, 97 Squadron and 166 Squadron, both then being employed in the training role as Bomber Command continued to expand in preparation for hostilities.

Leconfield was the airfield from where Bomber Command flew its first night operation of the war, a Nickelling sortie on the opening night of hostilities. But it was not the resident squadrons that flew this first mission. Being training units at the time, that task went instead to ten Whitley crews based at Linton-on-Ouse who flew the short distance to Leconfield to be loaded with propaganda leaflets, which they then dropped over Hamburg, Bremen and cities of the industrial Ruhr.

No aircraft were lost that opening night, although three were forced to land at airfields in France, but Leconfield's early involvement with Bomber Command was over. With 97 and 166 Squadrons having moved south, Leconfield was empty until October 1939, when the airfield was handed over to Fighter Command.

For the next couple of years Leconfield was home to Blenheims, Spitfires and Hurricanes. It was only after reconstruction work, carried out during 1942, that the airfield became a bomber base once more and transferred back to 4 Group. By then, Leconfield was a standard bomber airfield with three concrete runways (the main running in a near north-south direction) surrounded by a perimeter track, off which there were thirty-six aircraft dispersals and four maintenance hangars (there would eventually be five).

The first bombers arrived in December 1942. These were Wellingtons of 196 and 466 (RAAF) Squadrons. Both had recently formed at Driffield as squadrons of 4 Group and by the end of the year had completed the move to their new home at Leconfield.

The Aussies were under the command of their first CO, Wing Commander Reginald Bailey, one of only a handful of Australians posted to the new squadron when it had formed; the vast majority of the squadron's personnel were British or from other Commonwealth nations. Bailey would command the squadron for the next year as the number of Aussies on the squadron continued to grow.

466 was in bombing action for the first time on the night of 15/16 January 1943, when four of its aircraft joined a force of 157 bombers sent to attack the French Atlantic port of Lorient. It was just two nights after the squadron had made its operational debut, when six Wellingtons carried out a minelaying sortie off the Frisian Islands, and the night after the squadron had suffered its first casualties when an aircraft flown by 23-year-old Sergeant Ray Babington failed to return from another minelaying op. It is believed the Wellington was shot down by flak off Ameland, one of the West Frisian Islands off the northern coast of Holland.

At the end of January, the Aussies went to Germany for the first time. Then, on the night of 4/5 February, 196 Squadron flew its first op with eight of its aircraft joining another raid against Lorient. It was not long before the two Leconfield squadrons were ready to operate together and this occurred for the first time on the night of 5/6 March. The target was Essen and it was the opening night of the Battle of the Ruhr.

The Battle of the Ruhr proved to be a hard-fought campaign during which there were plenty of stories of personal courage. One example was on the night of 14/15 April. The target was Stuttgart and the raid involved a mixed force of 462 bombers, including the Wellingtons of 466 Squadron. One of the

Wellingtons was flown by Sergeant Edward Hicks. Having arrived over Germany his aircraft was attacked by an enemy night fighter. A devastating burst of fire left the rear gunner fatally injured and the bomb aimer, Pilot Officer Ray Hopkins, the navigator, Flying Officer Reg Clayton, and the wireless operator, Sergeant Fred Blair, all wounded.

It was chaos on board the Wellington but the situation was about to become worse when the night fighter closed for a second attack. Hicks did all that he could to fend off the attacker, manoeuvring the crippled bomber as hard and as best he could. It was a matter of life or death. With great skill, Hicks eventually threw off the night fighter and it was not to be seen again. Nonetheless, the bomber was crippled. Its hydraulic system had been ruptured, causing the wheels to come down and the bomb doors to open, but rather than turn back, a decision that would have been fully justified, Hicks and his crew decided to press on.

By now, Hopkins was struggling to maintain consciousness but he managed to direct his captain on to the target where the crew successfully released their bombs. Then, for more than two hours, the crew laboured their way back towards home while doing their upmost to keep the rear gunner alive. Eventually, the Wellington arrived back over England where it made an emergency landing. For their courage and determination that night, Hicks was awarded the CGM, Hopkins the DSO, Clayton the DFC and Blair the DFM. It was a rare occasion when four members of the same bomber crew were decorated for their courage during the same raid, and even more unusual was the fact that each had received a different decoration.

196 Squadron was now under the command of Wing Commander A G Duguid, who had taken over from the squadron's first CO, Wing Commander R H Waterhouse, in March. Leconfield's two squadrons continued with a mix of minelaying and bombing ops until June 1943 when 196 Squadron moved to Witchford in Cambridgeshire to convert to the Short Stirling, leaving the Australians to operate from Leconfield alone.

The Wellington had now reached the end of its operational life. It had been the work horse of Bomber Command since the opening day of the war but its capability had been surpassed by the newer four-engine heavy bombers that had entered service.

466 Squadron flew its last op with the Wellington at the end of August 1943.

During this period Leconfield was also briefly home to 1502 Beam Approach Training Flight before the unit disbanded in August, and to Mustangs of 170 Squadron during October – but only for forty-eight hours. It was now the turn of the Aussies of 466 Squadron to begin converting to the four-engine Halifax and so its crews went to Marston Moor and Riccall for conversion. The squadron was initially given Halifax IIs but these were exchanged for improved Mark IIIs by the time 466 was ready to commence operations at the beginning of December, just as the Battle of Berlin was getting fully underway.

At the beginning of 1944, Leconfield became home to a second Halifax unit when 640 Squadron was formed; its nucleus made up of crews from 466 Squadron and from 158 Squadron at Lissett. Leconfield would be 640's only home in what would turn out to be a short operational existence of a little more than a year.

The involvement of both Leconfield squadrons in the disastrous raid against Nuremberg on the last night of March 1944 resulted in very different outcomes; 466 came through unscathed while 640 lost three aircraft and crews, such was the nature of the air war over Germany and how luck often played its part.

When 466 Squadron moved back to Driffield during the first days of June 1944, 640 Squadron was left as Leconfield's only resident bomber squadron, although the airfield was also home to Oxfords of 1520 BATF until September when the flight moved out. During the supporting operations for D-Day, 6 June, 640 Squadron was involved in softening up the enemy coastal gun batteries in and around the Allied landing area, after which the squadron carried out numerous attacks against rail communications targets to prevent German troops from reaching the Normandy beachhead, and then carried out further attacks against the German V-weapon sites in northern France.

By the end of 1944 the strategic bombing campaign had returned to targets in Germany. Leconfield had now welcomed 96 Squadron of Transport Command, which immediately began converting to the Halifax for troop-carrying, although it would soon leave for the Far East. Then, in April 1945, the Halifaxes of 51 Squadron arrived from Snaith to fly its final operations of the war.

The former airfield of Leconfield is now Normandy Barracks, home to the Defence School of Transport. Grange Road leads down to the northern part of the airfield, at the end of which you can see hangars and the air traffic control tower off to the right. (Author)

Leconfield's two Halifax squadrons each sent eighteen aircraft on the Wangerooge raid on 25 April 1945. Then, once hostilities were over, 640 Squadron disbanded and Leconfield was transferred to Transport Command with 51 Squadron remaining for a few weeks before moving out.

Leconfield was retained by the post-war RAF and reverted to being a fighter station until the mid-1960s. Since then, part of the airfield was retained for a detachment of search and rescue helicopters but the main site was handed over to the army in 1977. It is now called Normandy Barracks and is home to the Defence School of Transport. Access to the camp is by prior permission only. However, Grange Road, which runs from the centre of the village of Leconfield, leads down to the northern part of the former airfield. It is a no-through road but at the end you can still see the hangars and air traffic control tower off to your right.

Summary of units based at Leconfield during the Second World War

97 Squadron (OF) – Jan 37 (Boscombe Down) – 16 Sep 39 (Abingdon)
Whitley II/III

166 Squadron (AS) – Jan 37 (Boscombe Down) – 16 Sep 39 (Abingdon)
Whitley I

196 Squadron (ZO) – 22 Dec 42 (Driffield) – 18 Jul 43 (Witchford)
Wellington X

466 (RAAF) Squadron (HD) – 27 Dec 42 (Driffield) – 2 Jun 44 (Driffield)
Wellington III (Oct – Dec 42)
Wellington X (Nov 42 – Sep 43)
Halifax II (Sep – Nov 43)
Halifax III (Nov 43 – Jun 44)

640 Squadron (C8) – 7 Jan 44 (Formed) – 7 May 45 (Disbanded)
Halifax III (Jan 44 – Mar 45)
Halifax VI (Mar – May 45)

96 Squadron (6H) – 30 Dec 44 (Odiham) – 25 Mar 45 (Far East)
Halifax III

51 Squadron (C6) – 20 Apr 45 (Snaith) – 20 Aug 45 (Stradishall)
Halifax III

CHAPTER 11

Lissett

Location – East Riding of Yorkshire, six miles south-west of Bridlington.
Status – Operational airfield. 43 Base – sub-station of Driffield.

Although land had been identified as early as 1941 as a potential satellite for the fighter airfield at Catfoss, Lissett was one of Yorkshire's last bomber airfields to be completed during the Second World War. The site was constrained by roads and a feature known as the Gransmoor Drain, but it was still possible to construct the airfield to the standard three-runway pattern design. The main was 1,900 yards long and orientated east–west, with two subsidiaries each of 1,400 yards, all connected by a perimeter track. There were thirty-six aircraft dispersals, two maintenance hangars and several temporary wartime buildings dispersed around the site with enough accommodation for more than 2,000 personnel. The technical site, including one of the two hangars, and the air traffic control tower were situated near the village of Lissett on what was the eastern side of the airfield.

Lissett opened in February 1943 as part of 4 Group, Bomber Command. Its first and only resident unit was 158 Squadron. Halifaxes arrived from Rufforth at the end of the month under the command of Wing Commander T R Hope, and the squadron flew its first operations from its new home on the night of 11/12 March. Ten of its aircraft joined another hundred Halifaxes, fifty Stirlings and more than 150 Lancasters in a raid against Stuttgart, but it was not a particularly successful start to the squadron's operational life at Lissett. Although the Pathfinders claimed to have successfully marked the target, the Main Force appears to have arrived late over the area. The German defences, which now included the use of decoys and dummy target indicators, meant that much of the bombing strayed towards the suburbs of the city and out into the open countryside. Eleven aircraft were lost on the raid, including one of 158's Halifaxes, that flown by 20-year-old Sergeant Harry Witham, with the loss of the entire crew.

The squadron had commenced operations from Lissett at what was the start of the Battle of the Ruhr. The campaign against the industrial targets of the Ruhr lasted until early July and was followed by the Battle of Hamburg during late-July and early-August, by which time the squadron was able to generate more than twenty aircraft for each raid. With better equipment and improved techniques, Bomber Command could now venture deeper into Nazi Germany but on the first main effort after the Hamburg offensive, a raid against Mannheim on the night of 9/10 August involving more than 450 aircraft, 158 Squadron lost its commanding officer. Hope's aircraft came down in Belgium; only he and two of his crew survived to become prisoners of war.

Command of the squadron now passed to Wing Commander C C Calder. Calder's first operation leading the squadron was the attack against the German V-weapons research establishment at Peenemünde on the Baltic coast. Twenty-four squadron aircraft took part in what turned out to be a successful raid, later said to have set the Nazi V-weapons programme back by at least two months. But the raid had been a costly one for Bomber Command. The forty aircraft lost that night included one from Lissett, that flown by 19-year-old Flight Sergeant William Caldwell from New Zealand, with the loss of all but one of his crew.

158 Squadron had become one of the biggest squadrons in 4 Group. Lissett's station commander during this period was Group Captain John Whitley, who had just returned to England having evaded capture. He had previously been the station commander of Linton-on-Ouse but had been shot down in April while flying as the second pilot in a Halifax of 76 Squadron. Whitley would soon be promoted to air commodore to command 43 Base, headquartered at Driffield but with Lissett as one of its sub-stations, and he would then be further promoted to air vice-marshal in February 1945 to become AOC 4 Group.

By the end of 1943, 158 Squadron had begun replacing its Halifax IIs with the Mark III. C Flight then formed the nucleus of a new Bomber Command squadron, 640 Squadron, under the command of Wing Commander D J H Eayrs, although this new squadron would take up residence at Leconfield. Meanwhile, 158 Squadron continued alone from Lissett throughout the hard winter of 1943/44, taking part in many raids against Berlin as well as the disastrous Nuremberg raid on the night of 30/31 March 1944. This latter raid, in particular, proved costly with the loss of four of the squadron's sixteen aircraft taking part. One of those was flown by Squadron Leader Sam Jones DFC, one of the flight commanders. The aircraft was shot down by flak and Jones is buried in the Rheinberg War Cemetery in Germany.

Although the Nuremberg raid had proved a disaster for Bomber Command and a bad night in general for Lissett, it had proved to be a lucky night for the crew of one Halifax of 158 Squadron. The aircraft was LV907, a new Halifax III carrying the squadron code 'NP-F'. Being on its first op, the aircraft had yet to be christened by the squadron. LV907 had only recently arrived from the factory and was flown to Nuremberg that night by Flight Sergeant Joe Hitchman, whose regular aircraft had been taken on the raid by Sam Jones who had been killed on the raid.

For Hitchman and his crew, it proved to be a lucky change of aircraft. They had returned safely from Nuremberg almost without incident and having survived its first op, LV907 was given the name 'F-Freddie'. The aircraft then became the regular mount of Pilot Officer Clifford 'Smithy' Smith. With the squadron having already lost seven aircraft carrying the code letter 'F-Freddie', Smith and his crew decided to give LV907 the 'unlucky' name of *Friday the Thirteenth*, with its nose art including an array of ill omens – including the skull and crossbones, an upside down horseshoe and the Grim Reaper – in the hope that it might break the previous jinx of the 'F-Freddies'. It worked. The now legendary LV907 went on to survive the war having safely completed 128 ops, the highest number of ops completed by any Halifax during the war. Its operational record had been set in just a matter of thirteen months. The aircraft was transported to London and put on public display in Oxford Street but, sadly, LV907 was later scrapped. It deserved far better.

With the Nuremberg raid having cost the squadron four of its aircraft, it would be a while before things would improve. In fact, things were not to get better for a while. Another disastrous night for Lissett was 2/3 June 1944 when five of 158 Squadron's aircraft failed to return. Bomber Command was supporting the final preparations for *Overlord,* and so its resources had been split to carry out attacks against a variety of targets in northern France. For Lissett's crews, the target was the railway marshalling yards at Trappes in the western suburbs of Paris. At that stage of the war the Germans were expecting the Allies to land in northern France but they did not know where. By destroying the marshalling yards, or at least by causing significant damage, it would prevent German reinforcements from reaching the Normandy beachhead. The raid was effectively an all-Halifax effort involving more than a hundred aircraft but the crews were met over the target area by several enemy night fighters. Fifteen of the Halifaxes were lost, including the five from 158 Squadron, making the overall loss rate for the raid over 14 per cent.

Fortunately for 158 Squadron, things were to improve in the months ahead as the Allies advanced towards Germany. Lissett was now commanded by Group Captain Alex 'Tom' Sawyer DFC, the former CO of 51 Squadron at Snaith with three operational tours behind him. But even as the war entered its final phase, Lissett received an unwelcome visitor. It was the night of 3/4 March 1945 when the Luftwaffe launched its Operation *Gisela,* a mass intruder raid by Ju 88s over eastern England. Lissett's crews were returning from a raid against a synthetic oil refinery at Bergkamen and were back in the vicinity of their home airfield when one of the Ju 88s struck. Its victim was the Halifax flown by 22-year-old Flight Lieutenant Chris Rogers, which came down in flames killing all on board. It was one of twenty RAF bombers shot down over English soil that night, leaving more than eighty men dead and many more injured.

Lissett's final operations of the war were flown on 25 April 1945 when 158 Squadron contributed twenty-seven aircraft to a large force of more than 300 Halifaxes sent to attack gun batteries on the Frisian island of Wangerooge. By the end of the war, some 250 operations had been flown from the airfield. Including losses due to training accidents or other incidents, 144

Halifaxes had been lost from Lissett with the loss of more than 400 lives.

With the war over, Lissett was transferred to Transport Command but after 158 Squadron left for Stradishall in August 1945, the airfield closed. As there was no place for Lissett in the post-war RAF, the land reverted to agriculture. The control tower was demolished long ago, although some of the buildings from the technical site remained intact for many years and used by farmers. However, there are very few reminders today of this once active bomber airfield. Although in existence for more than two years, facilities at the airfield were only ever considered basic at best. Most were accommodated in draughty Nissen huts but the airfield of Lissett seems to have been fondly remembered by those who served there. Maybe it was its close proximity to the east coast and the town of Bridlington that helped.

In more recent years, several wind turbines have been erected on the former airfield. The energy company, Novera Energy, included as part of its overall project the construction of a memorial to the 851 members of 158 Squadron who died in active service. In consultation with the 158 Squadron Association and the East Riding of Yorkshire Council, Novera held a design competition for the memorial. The winning entry was from a local artist, Peter Naylor. Unveiled in 2009, the memorial depicts seven bomber crew members in silhouette, with all 851 names etched on the figures, overlooking the former airfield from where they flew. It is a truly wonderful design.

The former airfield is on the west side of the A165 at the village of Lissett. When travelling south on the main road past the village, after about half a mile there is a turning off to the right. This takes you down to the perimeter track where many of the aircraft dispersals were located. More aircraft hard standings were further to the left around the perimeter track towards the south-west corner of the airfield while others, along with the bomb dump, were situated on the western side.

The main entrance to the wartime airfield was from Main Street in the village of Lissett. The memorial can be found by continuing along Main Street, which then becomes Gransmoor Road, and then continuing past Tithe Lane for a further 400 yards. The memorial can be seen on the left. It is signposted from the A165 at the village.

Overlooking the former airfield of Lissett is a wonderful memorial to 158 Squadron. It depicts seven members of a bomber crew, with 851 names of squadron members who died in active service etched on the figures, overlooking the airfield from where they flew. (Author)

Summary of units based at Lissett during the Second World War

158 Squadron (NP) – 28 Feb 43 (Rufforth) – 16 Aug 45 (Stradishall)
Halifax II (Feb 43 – Jan 44)
Halifax III (Jan 44 – Jun 45)
Halifax VI (Apr – Jul 45)

CHAPTER 12

Marston Moor (Tockwith)

Location – North Yorkshire, four miles north-east of Wetherby.
Status – Training airfield. HQ 41 Base.

Probably better known for its historic days of the English Civil War, Marston Moor was the focal point for the training of 4 Group's Halifax bomber crews during the Second World War. Located to the south-west of the village of Tockwith, the airfield is often referred to by the village name rather than Marston Moor on which the site was built.

Constructed to the standard three-runway bomber airfield design, Marston Moor opened in November 1941 as part of 4 Group, Bomber Command. The original intention had been for an operational bomber squadron to move in, but Marston Moor was instead established as a training base for 4 Group's new bomber crews to convert onto the Halifax heavy bomber.

In early 1942, the first Halifax Mark Is arrived from Leconfield to form 1652 Conversion Unit. This training unit would soon grow in size to become 1652 HCU with four flights of aircraft, although the HCU would generally be equipped with early marks of the Halifax that had been given up by the operational squadrons as they took delivery of newer variants.

With the exception of a few weeks during its first year, Marston Moor would be 1652's home for the rest of the war and together with 1658 HCU at Riccall, and 1663 HCU at Rufforth, these units carried the responsibility of converting all of 4 Group's Halifax crews onto type.

In April 1943 Marston Moor welcomed a notable figure when Leonard Cheshire arrived to take command of the station.

When Leonard Cheshire commanded Marston Moor in 1943 he was the RAF's youngest group captain at the age of twenty-five. But, being away from operations was not for him and so Cheshire took a reduction in rank to command 617 Squadron and was awarded the Victoria Cross in 1944 after completing his fourth tour of operations, totalling 100 operational sorties. It was the only time the VC was awarded for a period of prolonged operations rather than for a specific act. (AHB)

Cheshire was then the RAF's youngest group captain at the age of twenty-five and had some experienced men working under his command. One was the newly promoted Wing Commander David Wilkerson, who had earlier been awarded the DFC while serving with 35 Squadron and was now posted to Marston Moor as Training Inspector. He was responsible for the administrative control of the satellite airfields at Riccall and Rufforth before his return to operational flying.

Being a station commander was never going to suit a man like Cheshire and, being keen to return to operational flying, he pushed for a move away. In September he got his way and having taken a reduction in rank to wing commander, Cheshire left Marston Moor to take command of 617 Squadron at Coningsby in Lincolnshire and would later be awarded the Victoria Cross.

Being a training station, there were no shortage of accidents and incidents at Marston Moor. Flying was a dangerous occupation, even during training flights, particularly when flying a heavy bomber for the first time in bad weather or at night. With the RAF having re-organized its structure of airfields to a base system, Marston Moor became Headquarters 41 Base with its sub-stations at Riccall and Rufforth and a relief landing ground at Acaster Malbis.

Marston Moor was also home to some RAF fighters – Spitfires and Hurricanes – used for fighter affiliation training for the new bomber crews. At the end of 1944, the airfield was transferred to the new 7 (Training) Group, its training task continuing until the final weeks of the war, after which 1652 HCU disbanded. Then, with the arrival of Stirlings and Halifaxes of 1655 HCU, the airfield was briefly transferred to Transport Command before the HCU moved out at the end of 1945, after which Marston Moor closed.

With no requirement for Marston Moor in the post-war RAF, the airfield progressively ran down. It is now the site of Marston Moor Business Park and can be found by taking the B1224 York Road from Wetherby towards the village of Long Marston. About two miles short of Long Marston take a left turn into Roman Road, signposted to the business park. The turn-off to South Field Lane off to the right marks the area where the south-western threshold of the main runway once crossed the road. Following this lane takes you along the southern part of the former airfield to its most south-eastern extremity. Continuing northwards along Roman Road takes you through

Marston Moor Business Park, built on the former technical and administrative site, marks the north-western part of the former airfield. (Author)

the airfield's western boundary to its entrance; now the entrance to the business park. When driving through the park, there are indications that this was once part of the technical and administrative sites. The village of Tockwith marks the north-eastern corner of the former airfield.

Summary of units based at Marston Moor during the Second World War

1652 HCU – 2 Jan 42 – 25 Jun 45
Halifax

Chapter 13

Melbourne

Location – East Riding of Yorkshire, five miles south-west of Pocklington.
Status – Operational airfield. 44 Base – sub-station of Holme-on-Spalding Moor.

Located in the East Riding of Yorkshire near the village of Seaton Ross is the former wartime airfield of Melbourne. It was another of the county's bomber airfields to have only one resident squadron, 10 Squadron, and operated only one type of aircraft, the Halifax, during the Second World War, which is somewhat unusual given the length of time the airfield was in existence.

Soon after the outbreak of war, farm land to the south of the village of Melbourne was identified as suitable for the development of a grass relief landing ground for Leeming. Some temporary Nissen huts were put up for accommodation but there were no permanent buildings as such. Regular visitors during its early days were the Whitley Vs of 10 Squadron, then based at Leeming under the command of Wing Commander Sidney Bufton. There were even some operational sorties flown from Melbourne during this period but as soon as the bad weather came, the grass airfield at Melbourne was unsuitable for operations.

Being of little or no use during periods of bad weather, Melbourne was closed to flying to allow further construction work to be carried out. But with no operational squadron earmarked for Melbourne at that time, construction was slow and so the airfield was effectively dormant throughout 1941. Eventually, though, the airfield was brought up to the required standard for bomber operations, with three hardened runways.

A Halifax of 10 Squadron landing at Melbourne. The squadron was the airfield's only resident unit of the war. (IWM)

The main was 1,900 yards long and ran from the north-east of the airfield to the south-west. With two intersecting subsidiaries, each around 1,300 yards in length, the runways were linked by a hardened perimeter track, off which thirty-six aircraft hard standings were constructed, more than enough for a heavy bomber squadron, and enough accommodation for just over 2,000 personnel.

It had taken a long time to prepare the new airfield and although work was not complete, enough had been done by August 1942 to allow the airfield to be used by 10 Squadron once again. By now the squadron had converted to Halifax IIs and was under the command of the popular Wing Commander Dick Wildey DFC, but Melbourne's facilities were still not sufficient to conduct full operational turn-rounds of aircraft and so the Halifax crews soon became used to flying across to Pocklington to be bombed up prior to a mission.

Eventually, the technical site, complete with a hangar, was completed in the north-eastern part of the airfield. There were two more hangars on the eastern side of the airfield, while the southern part was used for bomb storage. It was not long before the squadron was ready to join 4 Group's major efforts but it was not to be a good start. Soon after it arrived at Melbourne, the squadron lost four of its Halifaxes during a raid on the town of Flensburg in northern Germany. It was the night of 1/2 October 1942 and a night when Bomber Command launched three relatively small-scale raids against Germany, carried out independently by 3, 4 and 5 Groups, all of which took part under difficult weather conditions and without support from the Pathfinders.

For the twenty-seven Halifax crews of 4 Group, including those from Melbourne, the night provided an opportunity to have another crack at Flensburg. An attempt the week before had resulted in a recall because of bad weather, while another attempt had proved costly; five of the twenty-eight aircraft involved were lost. However, this latest attempt on the opening night of October was to be no better. It would, in fact, be far worse. Twelve of the Halifaxes were lost, including four from Melbourne. Nearly half of the raiding force had failed to return, although those crews that had managed to reach the target had managed to achieve good bombing results.

Sadly, losses would continue and amongst those to lose his life while flying from Melbourne was 25-year-old Richard Wildey. He was killed later that month while leading the squadron on what turned out to be an unsuccessful raid on Cologne. Wildey was replaced by Wing Commander W Carter. Things then seemed to settle down before 10 Squadron's involvement in the hard-fought campaign against the industrial Ruhr during the spring of 1943, a campaign that saw eight of the squadron's aircraft fail to return during May and another five in June. The Battle of Hamburg followed and then it was the opening stages of the Battle of Berlin.

The Halifax crews were showing tremendous courage in the face of adversity and one example was that of the crew of Flight Lieutenant Jack Trobe, an Australian, during a raid on Düsseldorf on the night of 3/4 November 1943. Trobe's aircraft had been subjected to a series of attacks from enemy night fighters. It had been repeatedly hit and this resulted in the failure of two engines. This, in turn, had caused the failure of the aircraft's hydraulics, which meant the rear turret was out of action. But that was not the only problem. Three of the crew – the mid-upper gunner, the wireless operator and the flight engineer – had been wounded and the aircraft's intercom system and radio were out of action, making it impossible for the crew to communicate.

Despite all of this, Trobe had managed to flee the attackers and had got one of the engines to re-start. But there was carnage down the back of the fuselage. A fire had started near one of the turrets and so the flight engineer, Sergeant Bob Bridge, despite his wounds, crawled aft to assist the wounded mid-upper gunner, Flight Sergeant Bill Mowatt, and to quell the fire. Meanwhile, the wireless operator, Sergeant Tom Bisby, despite being in considerable pain from his own wounds, was busy trying to repair the radio set. Having succeeded to some degree, Bisby managed to obtain a vital fix to help Trobe set a course for home. They eventually made it back home where Trobe carried out a text book landing. For his superb leadership, Trobe was awarded the DFC, while Bisby was awarded the CGM and Mowatt and Bridge both received the DFM. It was a marvellous example of crew courage and co-operation to get a crippled bomber back to base. Trobe's citation concluded:

> *In the face of a perilous situation this officer displayed outstanding skill and courage and his valiant efforts were well supported by his comrades, whose courage, fortitude and devotion to duty were of a high order.*

10 Squadron was fully involved in the hard winter campaign of 1943/44 in what later became known as the Battle of Berlin. By the time it came to an end, the squadron had re-equipped with the Halifax III. The squadron was then involved in operations to support the Allied landings in Normandy, after which it carried out attacks against a variety of targets, including attacks against the many V-weapon sites that had now appeared in northern France. The Halifax proved to be such a versatile aircraft that in September Melbourne's aircraft were involved in transporting thousands of gallons of fuel to British forces in Belgium.

Melbourne was one of only two Yorkshire airfields to be installed with FIDO (see Carnaby for more about FIDO), but it was not installed and ready for use until late 1944 and so it is probably fair to say that FIDO was installed too late for many of Melbourne's crews who had been forced to divert elsewhere because of fog in the Vale of York. That said, once FIDO was

York Raceway uses a section of the former main runway for drag racing. Some of the wartime buildings have also survived in this north-eastern part of the airfield. (Author)

up and running, several 10 Squadron crews were grateful for it, as were crews from other Yorkshire squadrons when needing somewhere to land.

During the final weeks of the war, on the night of 3/4 March 1945, one of Melbourne's aircraft fell to the guns of a German Ju 88 night fighter near Knaresborough, having returned from a raid on the synthetic oil refinery at Bergkamen; it was another victim of the Luftwaffe's Operation *Gisela*. Finally, like most of Yorkshire's Halifax bases, Melbourne's last operation of the war was flown on 25 April 1945 against gun batteries on the Frisian island of Wangerooge.

With hostilities over, 10 Squadron was transferred to Transport Command. The majority of its 4,800 operational sorties, a record for 4 Group, had been flown from Melbourne, but success had come at a cost with 128 Halifaxes lost during the squadron's two and a half years operating from the airfield.

Melbourne was also briefly transferred to Transport Command. Another Dakota unit arrived but soon moved out and in early 1946, Melbourne closed. There were no plans for it in the post-war RAF and so the airfield gradually ran into disrepair. The land was then sold, although parts of the abandoned runways, perimeter track and hard standings, as well as many of the former wartime buildings, remained in use by local farmers for many years.

A brick memorial to 10 Squadron stands at the entrance to Melrose Farm, close to the old station entrance at the eastern part of the airfield. (Author)

This former wartime airfield is to the south-east of York, between the villages of Melbourne and Seaton Ross (its nearest village). When travelling north from Seaton Ross along Church Lane, which then becomes North End, the road eventually bears right into Mill Lane. On reaching a Y-junction, bear left and just over a hundred yards later there is a small turning off to the left. This is the eastern extremity of the former airfield and a brick memorial to 10 Squadron stands at the entrance to what is now Melrose Farm, close to the old station entrance. The memorial stands as a lasting tribute to those who served with the squadron at Melbourne during the Second World War. Continuing along the lane takes you to the northern extremity of the former airfield. This is where the administrative and technical sites once stood, and is now a farm. You will soon see a turning off to the left, which takes you down to York Raceway, which uses a section of the old main runway for drag racing. Some of the former wartime buildings in this area have also survived.

Summary of units based at Melbourne during the Second World War

10 Squadron (ZA) – 19 Aug 42 (Leeming) – 5 Aug 45 (Broadwell)
Halifax II (Aug 42 – Mar 44)
Halifax III (Mar 44 – Aug 45)

Chapter 14
Plainville

Location – North Yorkshire, five miles north of York.
Status – Advanced landing ground of Linton-on-Ouse.

Included amongst the many airfields of Yorkshire that were used by aircraft of Bomber Command during the Second World War is Plainville. Used as an advanced landing ground of Linton-on-Ouse, this grass airfield (although it was

Used as an advanced landing ground for Linton-on-Ouse, the grass airfield of Plainville was never used as an operational base but it was used during the early months of the war by Linton's Whitleys when there was a real threat of Bomber Command's main bases in Yorkshire coming under attack. However, beyond 1941 there was little, if any, use of the airfield as it was deemed unsuitable for further development. (via Ken Delve)

barely an airfield) was never an operational base. It was used, though, during the early years of the war by Linton's Whitleys of 58 Squadron at a time when there was a real threat of Bomber Command's main bases in Yorkshire coming under attack. However, beyond 1941 there was little, if any, use of the airfield. It was deemed to be unsuitable for further development and so its use gradually diminished and after the war the site reverted to the meadow that it once was.

The site of the former airfield is about five miles to the north of York and situated between the A19 and B1363 Sutton Road. From the A19 at Shipton by Beningbrough take East Lane, which then becomes Corban Lane. Follow Corban Lane eastwards for just over a mile and then turn left into Plainville Lane. This heads northwards and after about a mile it crosses a beck to become Bull Lane. At this point you are at the south-eastern corner of the former landing ground. Continuing along Bull Lane takes you along its eastern boundary. However, nothing of this former landing ground remains to be seen.

Chapter 15

Pocklington (Barmby)

Location – East Riding of Yorkshire on the western side of the town of Pocklington.
Status – Operational airfield. HQ 42 Base.

Another of Yorkshire's early airfields, Pocklington, or Barmby as it was originally known, dates back to the days of the Royal Flying Corps in the First World War. Knowing its background, it is not surprising that the site was surveyed during the mid-1930s as part of the RAF's Expansion Scheme, although, in the end, the new airfield of Pocklington was not built exactly on the original site but very near to the original aerodrome.

Although the location had been identified as suitable for development as a bomber airfield before the outbreak of the Second World War, it was not until after hostilities had commenced that work started on the site. The initial idea had been to develop an all-grass airfield but this was changed and so it was not until June 1941 that Pocklington finally opened.

Allocated to 4 Group, Pocklington was rather unique in that four hardened runways were constructed, although only three would be used. The reason for this was safety as the original main east–west runway ran too close to the village of Barmby Moor, and so a fourth runway, 1,800 yards long, was constructed at a slightly different angle and more towards the north-west. There were initially three hangars on the airfield, although three more would be erected later, making Pocklington's maintenance facilities very good for a wartime airfield. But its administrative and domestic accommodation, consisting mostly of draughty wooden buildings and Nissen huts, enough for nearly 2,000 personnel, were only ever considered to be basic to say the least.

Bombing up a Halifax II of 405 (Vancouver) Squadron RCAF at Pocklington during 1942. (IWM)

Pocklington would only ever accommodate one bomber squadron at any one time. Its first residents were Wellingtons of the newly formed 405 (Vancouver) Squadron RCAF, which immediately moved in from Driffield. At that time, the squadron was mixed in terms of its personnel's nationalities – British, Canadians and New Zealanders – but when the airfield first opened there was not enough accommodation for all and so some personnel found themselves billeted in the local area.

The squadron soon commenced operations from its new home and had the misfortune to suffer the RCAF's first loss in Bomber Command, when one of its Wellingtons failed to return from a raid on Cologne. One pilot serving with the squadron during those early days at Pocklington was John Searby, then aged twenty-eight and later to become a key figure in Bomber Command for his development of the Master Bomber concept.

The following February, Pocklington was used by a second Wellington squadron, the recently re-formed 158 Squadron, because facilities at its home base of Driffield were unserviceable.

158's Wellingtons became regular visitors to Pocklington to use 405's facilities and resources to re-fuel and re-arm.

405 Squadron flew its last Wellington operations on the night of 14/15 April 1942. The target was Dortmund and the squadron made up part of a mixed force of more than 200 aircraft sent to attack the city in Germany's industrial heartland of the Ruhr. The fact that five different types of bomber were involved in the raid – Wellingtons, Hampdens, Stirlings, Halifaxes and Manchesters – shows the diversity of Bomber Command at this time. Two-thirds of the force claimed to have bombed the target but the post-raid assessment showed bombing had been scattered over many miles. In addition to four Hampdens that failed to return, five Wellingtons were lost in the raid, including three from Pocklington. It was a sad end to the squadron's operational days with the Wellington.

405 Squadron then began its conversion to the newer and more capable Halifax II. A conversion flight was formed because Bomber Command had no conversion units at that stage. 405 then became the first Canadian squadron to take the Halifax into action when it took part in the first Thousand Bomber raid against Cologne at the end of May 1942; one of its aircraft failed to return. Conversion to the Halifax was soon complete but it had not been an easy start with the new type. By the end of its first month of operating the Halifax the squadron had lost ten aircraft, including three in one night.

405 Squadron's connection with Pocklington came to an end in August 1942 when it moved to Topcliffe, swapping places with another Halifax unit, 102 Squadron, which would now remain at Pocklington for the rest of the war. During its time at Pocklington, 405 had flown on more than eighty major raids and had lost twenty aircraft.

As part of the RAF's re-organization to a base structure, Pocklington became Headquarters 42 Base, with sub-stations at Elvington, Full Sutton and Melbourne, under the overall command of Air Commodore Gus Walker. Walker arrived in March 1943 having been the station commander at Syerston in Nottinghamshire. Known to those under his command as the 'one-armed bandit', he was already a legend in Bomber Command. It was while he was the station commander at Syerston that he had lost his right arm in a ground incident,

A Halifax II of 102 Squadron. The squadron replaced the Canadians of 405 Squadron in August 1942 and remained at Pocklington until the end of the war, although this picture was taken before this aircraft was lost in June 1943. (IWM)

having rushed to a burning Lancaster in the hope that he could rescue its crew before its bomb load exploded. However, the bombs detonated just as he was reaching the aircraft, catching him fully in the blast. Walker would remain at Pocklington as the base commander until February 1945 and his injury never held him back. He went on to enjoy an extremely successful post-war career in the RAF, later becoming AOC 1 Group and ultimately reaching the rank of air chief marshal.

102 Squadron quickly became immersed in Bomber Command's key strategic bombing campaigns against the Ruhr and Hamburg during 1943, followed by the Battle of Berlin during the hard and costly winter of 1943/44. One notable pilot to have flown with the squadron during the early part of this period was the highly decorated Squadron Leader Wally Lashbrook, who would later be awarded his Bomber Command clasp for his 1939–45 Star at the age of 100.

Lashbrook had joined the RAF as an aircraft apprentice and during his early days in the service had worked with an

When the RAF reorganized its airfields to a base structure in 1943, Pocklington became Headquarters 42 Base, with sub-stations at Elvington and Melbourne, all under the command of Air Commodore Gus Walker. Walker would remain in command of Pocklington until February 1945 and go on to enjoy a successful post-war career in the RAF, reaching the rank of air chief marshal. (AHB)

airman by the name of T E Shaw, better known by his real name of Thomas Edward Lawrence, the man now remembered as Lawrence of Arabia. By the time the Second World War had broken out, Lashbrook had trained as a pilot. As a sergeant pilot, he was awarded the DFM in April 1941 at the end of his tour flying Whitleys with 51 Squadron at Dishforth and while serving with 102 Squadron as a flight commander he added the DFC. But Lashbrook was then shot down during a raid on an armaments factory at Pilsen in Czechoslovakia on the night of 16/17 April 1943. Flying Halifax HR663 'DY-T', and having bombed the target, his aircraft was attacked on the way home by a Messerschmitt Bf 110 night fighter.

At the time the Halifax was over the Belgian–French border and although one of the gunners had been killed, Lashbrook and the rest of his crew managed to bale out. Two were captured but four evaded, including Lashbrook who was picked up by the French Resistance and returned home three months later by one of the aircrew escape lines, known as the Comet Line, which ran from Belgium through France and eventually to Spain. But having been exposed to the escape line, as well as other elements of the French Resistance, it was too risky for Lashbrook to return to bomber operations in case he was shot down again and so he saw out the rest of the war as a test pilot, adding an Air Force Cross (AFC) to his decorations as well as later being appointed as a Member of the Order of the British Empire.

102 Squadron was to lose many fine men during its time at Pocklington and one was its commanding officer, Wing Commander Bruce Bintley. Bintley's life came to an end on the night of 23/24 October, not over enemy territory but at nearby Holme-on-Spalding Moor (see Holme-on-Spalding Moor for details of his death). It was a sad loss; Bintley had been a popular CO.

Sadly, there were to be many more losses for the squadron. One raid, in particular, resulted in heavy losses. It was a raid against the Nazi capital, flown during the height of the Battle of Berlin on the night of 20/21 January 1944, when five of 102's sixteen Halifaxes failed to return and two more crashed in England. And if this was not bad enough for those at Pocklington at the time, four more of the squadron's aircraft were lost the following night during a raid against Magdeburg.

Despite these losses, the squadron was soon sending more than twenty aircraft on a raid and was fortunate to escape the mauling by German night fighters during Bomber Command's disastrous raid on Nuremberg at the end of March 1944.

As the war entered its final year Pocklington was fully involved in the build-up to Operation *Overlord* with 102 Squadron joining the other Halifax squadrons of 4 Group to carry out attacks against railyards and other important lines of communications in northern France. Then, on the eve of D-Day, the squadron sent twenty-six aircraft, its largest effort so far, to bomb an enemy gun battery on the Normandy coast. However, even as the Allies began to break out from the beachhead into northern France, the squadron's losses continued, reminding everyone at Pocklington that the war was far from over.

First, five of 102's Halifaxes were lost on the night of 16/17 June during a raid against a synthetic oil plant at Sterkrade and then five more of Pocklington's Halifaxes failed to return from a raid against railway marshalling yards in northern France on the night of 28/29 June. This latter raid involved 200 Halifaxes from 4 and 6 Groups, supported by Pathfinder Lancasters of 8 Group, and the plan was for Bomber Command to split its resources to attack yards at Blainville and Metz. The 102 crews were involved in the 4 Group attack on Blainville but eleven Halifaxes, including the five from Pocklington, were lost that night. The crews of 6 (RCAF) Group had also suffered with seven aircraft failing to return, while the Pathfinders lost two Lancasters; one from each raid. It was a bad night for everyone involved.

Having upgraded to the Hercules-powered Halifax Mark III, 102 Squadron, like many of Yorkshire's Halifax squadrons, was involved in the airlift of petrol to Belgium during September 1944 to support the British Second Army. In the space of just one week the squadron's Halifaxes lifted well over 100,000 gallons of fuel. Then, on 14/15 October, the squadron's crews took part in operations against Duisburg, with many crews flying two missions within the space of just a few hours: one by day and the other by night. No aircraft from Pocklington were lost.

During the final weeks of the war, the squadron began taking delivery of the Halifax VI to work alongside the Mark IIIs. Like most other Halifax squadrons, 102's last raid of the war was flown on 25 April 1945 against gun batteries on the Frisian island of Wangerooge.

With the war over, 102 Squadron was transferred to Transport Command and left for Bassingbourn in September, giving up its Halifaxes along the way for the American-built Consolidated B-24 Liberator. With its squadron gone, Pocklington was briefly home to an aircrew holding unit. The airfield was retained as an emergency landing ground, but the truth was that it lacked the facilities required to have a future in the post-war RAF, and so Pocklington closed to flying in 1946, after which the land gradually reverted to agriculture.

This airfield can be found adjacent to the western side of the town of Pocklington between the A1079 York Road and the B1246. The runways are still used by the Wolds Gliding Club while the former technical and administrative sites were developed into the Pocklington industrial estate, with its access roads given appropriate names, such as Halifax Way and Wellington Road.

When travelling from the direction of York along the A1079, the entrance to this area is from a roundabout signposted left for the town of Pocklington. Having turned off the main road at the roundabout, bear immediately left at the mini-roundabout

In 1985, a memorial to the two squadrons that served at Pocklington during the Second World War was unveiled by Air Chief Marshal Sir Gus Walker. The memorial can be found outside the gliding club. (Author)

into Halifax Way and this takes you through the area that was once used as the technical and administrative sites. However, if you bear right at the mini-roundabout instead, into Hodsow Lane, this lane continues towards Pocklington and the turning for the gliding club is soon found on your left. A memorial to Pocklington's two wartime bomber squadrons stands outside the gliding club. It was unveiled in 1985 by Air Chief Marshal Sir Gus Walker, who had been Pocklington's base commander for the last two years of the war.

Summary of units based at Pocklington during the Second World War

405 (Vancouver) Squadron RCAF (LQ) – 20 Jun 41 (Driffield) – 6 Aug 42 (Topcliffe)
Wellington II (Jun 41 – Apr 42)
Halifax II (Apr – Aug 42)

102 Squadron (DY) – 7 Aug 42 (Topcliffe) – 7 Sep 45 (Bassingbourn)
Halifax II (Aug 42 – May 44)
Halifax III (May 44 – Sep 45)
Halifax VI (Jul – Sep 45)

CHAPTER 16

Riccall

Location – North Yorkshire, four miles north-east of Selby. Status – Training airfield. 41 Base – sub-station of Marston Moor.

Constructed as a satellite of Marston Moor, Riccall was built on common land with three concrete runways, albeit with a slightly unusual layout because of the constraints of the land. The main runway, 2,000 yards long, ran from the north-east corner of the airfield to the south-west, but its threshold in the south-west part of the airfield met a second runway aligned almost north–south. Also meeting this second runway at a point slightly further to the north was the airfield's third runway, which ran from that point in an almost easterly direction. A hardened perimeter track linked the runways with the technical sites being situated on the northern and eastern parts of the airfield.

The airfield was first used during the latter half of 1942 by Halifaxes based at Linton-on-Ouse. Linton's resident squadrons were then 76 and 78 Squadrons and the conversion flights from each of these squadrons were regular visitors to the new airfield before they were combined to form 1658 HCU at Riccall in October 1942.

Riccall would be 1658's home for the rest of the war and the HCU was soon expanded to four flights of more than thirty aircraft, with the task of training Halifax crews for the frontline squadrons of 4 Group. But not all the crews coming through the training system were brand-new sprog crews. As Bomber Command replaced its Wellington squadrons with the newer four-engine Halifax, the HCU took these operationally experienced crews through a shortened conversion course.

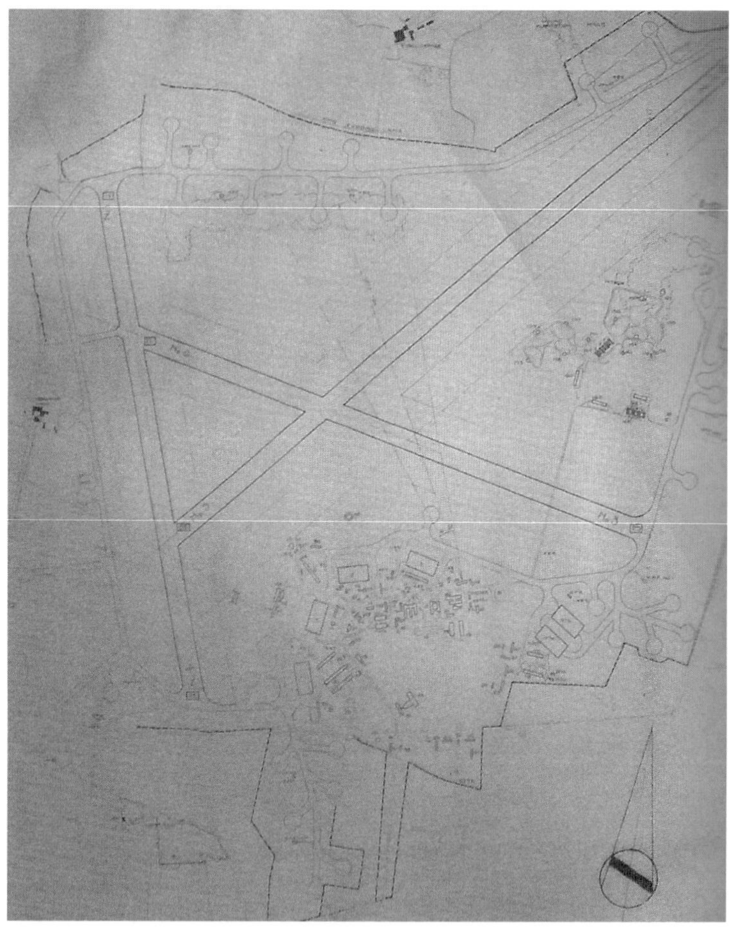

Wartime layout of Riccall, a training airfield and satellite of Rufforth, and home to Halifaxes of 1658 HCU from October 1942 until the final days of the war. (via Ken Delve)

Furthermore, a crew's conversion onto the Halifax included the addition of a flight engineer, a position not required in the Wellington and brought about because of the complexities of the new four-engine heavy bombers entering operational service.

As with any training airfield, there was no shortage of accidents, which was never helped by the fact that the HCU's aircraft were often old and tired with few, if any, modifications or new equipment to help the crews when flying in bad weather or at night.

As part of the RAF's re-organization of its airfields in 1943, Riccall became a sub-station of 41 Base, headquartered at Marston Moor. This administrative change made little or no difference to the HCU. Now under the command of the experienced Halifax pilot, Wing Commander Henry Drummond DFM, who had earlier flown an operational tour as a sergeant pilot with 76 Squadron at Middleton St George, the training task continued as normal into the following year. Drummond was awarded the AFC for his leadership of the HCU and, like other RAF training airfields, Riccall was transferred to 7 (Training) Group at the end of 1944.

As the war drew towards a close the training requirement reduced and then ceased altogether, leading to the HCU disbanding just before the end of the war. During its time at Riccall, 1658 HCU had lost more than seventy aircraft due to flying accidents.

Riccall was then briefly transferred to Transport Command but by the end of 1945 it had closed to flying. The site was initially retained by the post-war RAF and used for storage purposes, but the land soon reverted to agriculture with many former airfield buildings being used by farmers or for other purposes. Part of the land was also used for a while for mining, but the land has now mostly reverted to farming with there being few reminders of this once active airfield.

The site can be found to the south-east of Riccall, east of the A19 and bordering the western side of Skipwith Common nature reserve. When travelling north along the A19 from Selby, the A163 Market Weighton Road heads eastwards along the southern boundary of the former airfield. A turning left into the industrial estate takes you to the areas of the former technical and administrative sites. This also marks the area where the eastern end of one of the subsidiary runways (29/11) was located.

By continuing along the A19 north towards York (rather than turning onto the A163 towards Market Weighton), you will see on your left the turning to the village of Riccall but immediately past this turning is a turn-off to the right called King Rudding Lane. Following this lane takes you through the northern part of the former airfield. After just over a mile you will first cross the

An old propeller stands as a memorial to those who served at Riccall during the Second World War. It can be found where the bomb dump was located, now part of the Skipwith Common National Nature Reserve. (Author)

old perimeter track and then cross what was the main runway. Continuing eastwards along the lane takes you into Skipwith Common National Nature Reserve. This is where the bomb dump was situated. A memorial in the shape of an old propeller was erected in 2010 to those who served at Riccall during the war. It is not easily found, though. You will need to continue some way into the nature reserve until you come to a T-junction with two gated tracks ahead of you – known locally as five-ways. The gates are locked to vehicles but taking the right of the two tracks leads you down to the memorial, which can be found less than a hundred yards away.

Summary of units based at Riccall during the Second World War

1658 HCU – 7 Oct 42 – 13 Apr 45
Halifax

Chapter 17
Rufforth

Location – North Yorkshire, two miles west of York.
Status – Operational and then a training airfield. 41 Base – sub-station of Marston Moor.

Built to the standard bomber airfield design with three hardened runways (the longest being 2,000 yards long and aligned north-east to south-west), three hangars and enough accommodation for nearly 1,800 personnel, Rufforth opened in November 1942. The airfield had already been used on occasions by conversion flights of nearby squadrons, but Rufforth had been built with training in mind. That said, its first resident unit was 158 Squadron, which moved in from East Moor within days of the new airfield's formal opening.

158's stay at Rufforth would be short but the squadron wasted no time and commenced operations from its new home almost straight away. It was the night of 7/8 November 1942 and the target was the Italian city of Genoa. Eight of Rufforth's Halifaxes made up part of a mixed force of 175 aircraft. The raid seemed to be a success but Genoa was on the limit of the aircraft's range. The crews found the combination of the long distance across the Alps to the target and the difficult wind conditions encountered on their way home, a major problem and this meant that only one of the squadron's aircraft made it back to Rufforth. The other seven were all forced to land wherever they could. One had run out of fuel over the sea and had no option other than to ditch in the Humber estuary after being airborne for more than eleven hours. Tragically, three of the crew drowned.

In the space of just nine days the squadron went to Genoa three times, each time proving difficult for the crews taking part. Only two of the six aircraft taking part in the third of these raids,

A Halifax of 1663 HCU pictured at Rufforth during the hard winter of 1943/44. (AHB)

flown on the night of 15/16 November, made it back to Rufforth, the shortage of fuel again being the problem.

It had not been an easy start to life at Rufforth for 158 Squadron and things during early 1943 were to be little better, with several losses before the squadron moved to the new airfield at Lissett. During its short stay at Rufforth, the squadron had lost nine aircraft and more than sixty men.

With the departure of 158 Squadron, the role of Rufforth changed to training and conversion to the Halifax. The airfield's short operational life was over. In March 1943, 1663 HCU formed at Rufforth and it was not long before the airfield was home to more than thirty aircraft, mostly Halifax IIs but latterly some Mark Vs as well.

One young sergeant pilot to pass through the HCU during this period was 22-year-old Cyril Barton, later to become 4 Group's only VC winner of the war. Barton had completed his flying training under the Arnold Scheme in America and after his Halifax conversion at Rufforth he was briefly posted to 78 Squadron at Breighton before being commissioned and posted to 578 Squadron at Burn (see Burn for details of Barton's VC).

As part of the RAF's re-organization of airfields during 1943, Rufforth became a sub-station of 41 Base, headquartered at

Marston Moor. This administrative change made no difference to the role of Rufforth and it continued to convert bomber crews to the Halifax for the rest of the war. By the summer of 1944 a few Spitfires and Hurricanes had also arrived at Rufforth to provide fighter affiliation training for the bomber crews. Then, in November, as with Yorkshire's other training airfields, Rufforth was transferred to 7 (Training) Group.

As the war drew to a close, the requirement to convert crews to the Halifax reduced and once hostilities were over the HCU disbanded. Rufforth may not have been an operational airfield since the early days of 1943, but it had suffered its fair share of losses. As with all training airfields during the Second World War, flying accidents were all too frequent, particularly when new crews were flying ageing aircraft around the high areas of the nearby York Moors and Pennines in poor weather. Rufforth had suffered some sixty accidents in the last two years.

Although Rufforth did not feature heavily in the post-war RAF, the airfield was retained for a number of years before it closed in the late-1950s. The hangars and wartime buildings gradually disappeared but part of the former airfield remained intact and used for a variety of purposes over the years. Part of the site was known for many years as the Rufforth Circuit, with

Now lying in a derelict state, the former control tower at Rufforth presents a rather sad sight. At least it is still standing – just – but it is on private property and so cannot be seen without prior permission. (Author)

Looking along Runway 17 at Rufforth, now used by the York Gliding Centre. (Author)

a two-mile length of motor racing track, but this was abandoned in the late-1970s.

Today, this former wartime bomber airfield is part privately owned, part home to the York Gliding Centre (which operates from the western part of the airfield) and part home to Airsports Training, a centre of excellence in microlight pilot and instructor training, which operates on the eastern part of the airfield. The former air traffic control tower is situated on the part that is privately owned but, disappointingly, has been left derelict for many years.

The airfield can be found two miles west of York, to the south of Rufforth village and on the south side of the B1224. Access to Airsports Training is from the B1224, but for the York Gliding Centre access is from Bradley Lane, which runs south from the village of Rufforth along the western boundary of the airfield. This is where most of the wartime aircraft dispersals were once situated. You will then see a turning to the York Gliding Centre, which marks the south-west corner of the airfield.

Summary of units based at Rufforth during the Second World War

158 Squadron (NP) – 6 Nov 42 (East Moor) – 27 Feb 43 (Lissett)
Halifax II

1663 HCU (OO/SV) – Mar 43 (Formed) – May 45 (Disbanded)
Halifax II/V

CHAPTER 18

Snaith (Pollington)

Location – East Riding of Yorkshire, nine miles east of Pontefract.
Status – Operational airfield.

Home for two bomber squadrons during its four years of war – 150 and 51 Squadrons – Snaith was another of Yorkshire's airfields to have its origins dating back to before the Second World War. But, although land to the west of Goole had been identified as suitable for development before hostilities had broken out, it was not until 1940 that work began. Because of many local geographic features, the new airfield had to be built between a canal (then the Knottingley and Goole Canal), a main road (the A645) and a major railway line (the main east coast line connecting London and the North-East).

The airfield was called Snaith rather than Pollington, after the village nearby, to avoid potential confusion with another new airfield being built in Yorkshire called Pocklington. Snaith was constructed as a standard bomber airfield with three concrete runways, the main being nearly 1,900 yards long and running east–west, and two subsidiaries, each about 1,400 yards long, all connected by a perimeter track. Three maintenance hangars and a technical site were built on the southern side of the airfield near the canal.

By the summer of 1941 the airfield was considered ready for opening and was initially allocated to 1 Group, Bomber Command. Within days, its first resident unit moved in. This was 150 Squadron, a Wellington squadron, which moved in during July, and for more than a year the squadron operated alone from Snaith until it moved out in October 1942 in preparation for a move to North Africa; its last operation from Snaith was

Halifax of 51 Squadron at Snaith. (via Ken Delve)

flown on the night of 23/24 October, when six aircraft carried out minelaying off the Danish coast with one aircraft failing to return.

The Wellingtons were immediately replaced by Halifaxes of 51 Squadron. This squadron had earlier been equipped with Whitleys and temporarily loaned to Coastal Command, but its move to Snaith signalled a change in aircraft as the squadron reverted back to a bombing role, with the first of its new four-engine heavies arriving during November.

Now home to a Halifax squadron, Snaith was transferred to 4 Group and would be 51 Squadron's home for the rest of the war. On the evening of 13 February 1943, the Halifaxes were bombed up ahead of what would be Bomber Command's heaviest raid of the war on the French Atlantic port of Lorient. Being the winter, take-off was early and so it was around 5.30 p.m. when the crew of one aircraft, DT722 'MH-M', were stood around their aircraft waiting to climb on board. They were chatting to another crew from the Halifax parked nearby and as there were a few moments to spare the bomb aimer climbed aboard 'MH-M' to make a final check of the bomb circuitry. He then joined his colleagues once more but just a few minutes later smoke was seen to be coming from the aircraft's bomb bay. Knowing that an explosion might be imminent, the crews fled to safety and took cover in some nearby trees.

The alarm had been raised and amongst those rushing to the scene was the squadron commander, Tom Sawyer. By the time they arrived the fire had taken hold and the aircraft soon burned out. Another crew at a distant dispersal had already climbed aboard their aircraft and on connection of the aircraft's batteries, a bunch of incendiaries fell from the aircraft. A fire started and soon the crew had vacated their aircraft. Everyone else in the area ran for cover as a bomb went off, the result being that another Halifax had soon burned out.

The squadron's involvement in the operation was cancelled for that night while an engineering investigation looked into why this had happened. The aircraft were still new and it turned out that remnants from the drilling of the bomb panel during manufacture had caused a short circuit; the consequence being that when the bomb switch was selected to 'safe' it released the aircraft's bomb load! All similar aircraft were checked and any faults rectified, but there were no further incidents. It had, however, been a scare for those involved. Several airmen were injured that night, some of whom were mentioned in despatches for their bravery in evacuating the scene and fighting the fires.

Fortunately, despite arming several aircraft every night in preparation for ops, ground incidents such as this were few and far between. Nonetheless, when there were incidents ground personnel were often injured or even killed as a result, and such occurrences provided a reminder to all ground personnel at RAF stations that operating armed aircraft during a time of war was dangerous.

51 Squadron's crews took part in most of Bomber Command's major efforts throughout 1943 before converting to the Halifax III at the beginning of 1944. Also in January 1944, 578 Squadron was formed at Snaith as part of 4 Group. 578 was yet another new squadron to form as Bomber Command continued to expand. Essentially made up of crews from part of 51 Squadron, the new squadron was ready to commence operations almost immediately. It was the height of the Battle of Berlin and so 578 Squadron flew its first operation on the night of 20/21 January. Five of its aircraft made up part of a large force of 769 aircraft sent to the Nazi capital.

It was never planned for 578 Squadron to stay at Snaith for long and having reached its establishment it moved out to Burn the following month where it would spend the rest of the war. Once again, 51 Squadron was alone at Snaith. The squadron suffered particularly badly during the disastrous raid against Nuremberg on the last night of March 1944. 51 had contributed seventeen aircraft to the raid but six failed to return; five were shot down over Europe while the sixth crash-landed back in England. One-third of the squadron had been lost in a single night.

It was not long before another squadron arrived at Snaith, albeit for just a week, but the new arrivals were not more bombers. They were Typhoons of 266 Squadron, which detached to Snaith from their base at Needs Oar Point in the New Forest at the end of April to prepare for their role in support of the forthcoming Normandy landings. During its stay the squadron pilots worked with the army to practise close air support, a role that would be crucial during the Allied landings.

With the Typhoons gone, 51 Squadron continued alone from Snaith until the final days of the war when it moved to Leconfield. But the last days of operating from Snaith were not without loss and one Halifax crew to be killed in the final days was that of NP932 'MH-J', flown by 22-year-old Flying Officer Stan Chopping from Bournemouth, which crashed on the airfield having returned from a raid on Homberg during the night of 14/15 March 1945. Homberg had

The last days of operations from Snaith were not without loss and one to lose his life during the final weeks of the war was Flying Officer Stan Chopping. His Halifax crashed on the airfield having returned from a raid on Homberg in March 1945. Chopping's crew were also killed. (Jacqui Watts)

been the crew's twenty-fourth op and for the Chopping family it was another sad loss. Squadron Leader Ralph Chopping DFC had been killed in August 1944, also while serving with Bomber Command.

With its aircraft gone, Snaith closed to flying, although it was briefly home to an aircrew holding unit. During Snaith's operational existence more than 200 aircraft had been lost from the airfield with the loss of more than a thousand lives. One of the most famous Halifaxes to have flown from the airfield was LV937. Having initially flown with 578 Squadron as 'LK-X' and then 'LK-R', LV937 was then transferred to 51 Squadron and as 'MH-E', known affectionately to the crews as 'Expensive Babe', completed at least a hundred operational sorties with the squadron.

Snaith briefly re-opened to flying during late-1945 and early-1946 when Airspeed Oxfords of 1516 Beam Approach Training Flight arrived but once the flight disbanded the airfield closed to flying once again. Having no future with the post-war RAF, Snaith lay dormant for several years. Eventually, the runways were dug up when the M62 was built.

The site of the former wartime airfield is effectively bisected by the M62. If heading eastbound towards Hull, it is after the

A beautifully maintained memorial garden near the village of Pollington stands on what was the southern part of the former airfield of Snaith and marks where the administrative and technical sites once stood. (Author)

exit for the A19 but before the exit for the M18. To view the area in more detail, take the Pontefract Road south-west from the town of Snaith. After about a mile, this road runs parallel to the M62 motorway to become Broach Road and you are now passing through the northern part of the former airfield. Turning left into Long Lane takes you under the motorway and at Great Heck the road becomes Heck and Pollington Lane. This is the western extremity of the former airfield. Follow the lane eastwards and after about a mile, just before reaching the village of Pollington, you will see an entrance into the Kelkay sand and gravel yard on your left. Turn left here and you will soon see a memorial garden on your left, immediately past the entrance to the staff car park. This is the southern part of the former airfield and marks where the administrative and technical sites once stood. There are many individual memorials to be seen. It is a really beautifully maintained garden and a pleasure to visit.

Summary of units based at Snaith during the Second World War

150 Squadron (JN) – 10 Jul 41 (Newton) – 26 Oct 42 (Kirmington)
Wellington I (Jul 41 – Jun 42)
Wellington III (Apr – Dec 42)

51 Squadron (MH) – 27 Oct 42 (Chivenor) – 19 Apr 45 (Leconfield)
Halifax II (Nov 42 – Jan 44)
Halifax III (Jan 44 – Apr 45)

578 Squadron (LK) – 14 Jan 44 (Formed) – 5 Feb 44 (Burn)
Halifax III

PART II

Airfields of 6 (RCAF) Group

Formed on 1 January 1943, 6 (RCAF) Group, or the Canadian Bomber Group as it is sometimes called, was a unique organization within Bomber Command by virtue of its nationality and the fact that the Canadian Government met the cost of the group with the exception of the pay and allowances of the small number of its non-Canadian personnel.

6 (RCAF) Group was the most northerly of Bomber Command's operational groups. Headquartered at Allerton Park, an old Victorian castle to the east of Knaresborough, its first AOC was Air Vice-Marshal George Brookes, who had arrived in the UK on promotion after commanding a training group in Canada. To get a new group up and running was never going to be easy, and so Brookes had taken up his appointment more than two months earlier and had already established many of his headquarters staff.

Brookes was given a healthy start. The RAF initially transferred six of its operational bomber airfields in Yorkshire and County Durham to the new group – Croft, Dalton, Dishforth, Leeming, Middleton St George and Topcliffe – with a seventh, Skipton-on-Swale, still under construction. With these airfields came eight operational squadrons of the RCAF – 408, 419, 420, 424, 425, 426, 427 and 428 – with a ninth (405) soon coming on board after its attachment to Coastal Command.

Being established with operational squadrons and crews meant that 6 (RCAF) Group was ready to commence operations immediately, and flew its first op on the night of 3/4 January 1943 when six Wellingtons of 427 (Lion) Squadron RCAF based at Croft took part in minelaying operations off the Frisian Islands.

Then, on the night of 14/15 January, the new group flew its first bombing missions of the war when fourteen of its Wellingtons were part of a force of more than 120 aircraft sent to attack the German U-boat submarine base at the French port of Lorient. This night also marked the group's first operational loss when a Wellington of 426 (Thunderbird) Squadron went missing with the loss of the entire crew.

During those early days the group's squadrons were mostly equipped with Wellingtons, although three (405, 408 and 419) had already converted to the Halifax. The group soon started to grow in size and along came more airfields – East Moor, Linton-on-Ouse and Wombleton – as 6 (RCAF) Group, like the rest of Bomber Command, restructured under a new base system. More squadrons came too (429, 431, 432, 433 and 434), although three of the group's original squadrons (420, 424 and 425) were briefly transferred to North Africa during the latter half of 1943 before returning to 6 (RCAF) Group at the end of the year. The last squadron to join the group was 415 (Swordfish) Squadron RCAF, which joined Bomber Command in July 1944.

All of the Canadian squadrons converted to four-engine heavies, mostly Halifaxes, as command of the group passed

A Halifax of 408 (Goose) Squadron RCAF. At the peak of its strength in early 1945, the all-Canadian 6 (RCAF) Group had fourteen operational squadrons, some of which had converted to the Lancaster, with two squadrons at each of the group's seven main operating bases – Croft, East Moor, Linton-on-Ouse, Leeming, Middleton St George, Skipton-on-Swale and Tholthorpe – all in, or just beyond, the Vale of York. (AHB)

to Air Vice-Marshal Clifford McEwan, a forceful and dynamic leader known as 'Black Mike'. McEwan had taken over during the height of the Battle of Berlin when the German night fighter force was at the peak of its effectiveness. Casualties amongst the group's bomber crews were high and so one of McEwan's first tasks was to try and bring the figure down by introducing a training programme for all of his crews, regardless of their background or experience.

While this was not particularly popular amongst many of the more experienced campaigners, it seemed to work and the casualty rate reduced. Furthermore, according to Ministry of Defence figures, aircraft serviceability was maintained at an average of 80 per cent for the rest of the war, enabling the group to fly in excess of 25,000 operational sorties. More than 86,000 tons of bombs and mines were dropped during 1944, and during one month alone after D-Day the group flew 3,740 operational sorties and dropped 13,274 tons of bombs. Its biggest effort of the war was on the night of 6/7 October 1944 when 6 (RCAF) Group contributed 293 aircraft (248 Halifaxes and 45 Lancasters) of the 523 aircraft sent to Dortmund to open what was a new campaign against the industrial Ruhr. Only two of the group's aircraft were lost, a remarkably low figure for such a large attacking force.

At the peak of its strength in early 1945, 6 (RCAF) Group had grown to fourteen operational squadrons, some of which had converted to Lancasters, with two squadrons at each of the group's seven main operating bases – Croft, East Moor, Linton-on-Ouse, Leeming, Middleton St George, Skipton-on-Swale and Tholthorpe – all of which were in, or just beyond, the Vale of York.

6 (RCAF) Group's final mission of the war was flown on 25 April 1945 against gun batteries on the Frisian island of Wangerooge, bringing to an end the massive contribution of the group, which had seen the Canadian squadrons fly more than 40,000 operational sorties, during which in excess of 125,000 tons of bombs had been dropped.

With hostilities over, 6 (RCAF) Group was involved in the repatriation of Allied prisoners of war. Furthermore, the war was still raging in the Far East and so eight of its squadrons were earmarked for Tiger Force. These flew to Canada to prepare for

A memorial dedicated to the men and women of 6 (RCAF) Group can be found at the Yorkshire Air Museum, located on the former wartime bomber airfield of Elvington. (Author)

their move out to the Pacific, while four squadrons remained in Yorkshire with Bomber Command, another was transferred to Transport Command and one was disbanded. But after the Japanese surrender brought war in the Far East to an end, 6 (RCAF) Group disbanded. Its badge is appropriately designed with a maple leaf superimposed on a York rose to symbolize the close link between the Canadians and the county of Yorkshire.

Chapter 19

Croft

Location – County Durham, five miles south of Darlington. Status – Satellite airfield. 64 (RCAF) Base – sub-station of Middleton St George.

Situated just to the south of the market town of Darlington in County Durham is the former wartime bomber airfield of Croft. Otherwise known to the locals as Neasham, the airfield was Bomber Command's second most northerly of the Second World War.

Land had been identified adjacent to the main east coast railway line, connecting London and the north-east of England and Scotland, and on the west side of the A167 Northallerton–Darlington road. Following the compulsory purchase by the government of 160 acres of farmland, work began during 1940 but it wasn't until nearly the end of the following year that the airfield was completed to the standard bomber design.

Halifaxes of 431 (Iroquois) Squadron RCAF pictured during 1944. By the end of the year Croft would be one of three airfields belonging to 6 (RCAF) Group to have converted to the Lancaster. (via Ken Delve)

Croft was officially opened in October 1941 as a satellite of Middleton St George, the furthest north of Bomber Command's airfields, and allocated to 4 Group. Croft's first arrivals were Whitley Vs of 78 Squadron under the command of Wing Commander Basil Robinson, which arrived from Middleton the same month. The new arrivals were soon in action and the squadron lost its first aircraft on the opening night of November during a raid against the German port of Kiel. Thirty Whitleys joined a mixed-force of 134 aircraft (including Wellingtons and Hampdens) to attack targets in the harbour. One of Croft's Whitleys failed to return.

The weather during those early winter months of operating from Croft made life difficult at times for the Whitley crews. Being so far north, it was already evident they would struggle to get home from targets deep in Germany, particularly when bad weather meant they needed to recover with enough spare fuel to divert elsewhere if required.

Basil Robinson was awarded the DFC for leading the squadron during a daylight raid against the German battleships *Scharnhorst* and *Gneisenau* at Brest on 18 December. Always keen to fly on operations whenever the opportunity presented itself, Robinson would later add a Bar to his DFC and a DSO but he

A Halifax of 434 (Bluenose) Squadron RCAF, Croft's other resident squadron during the latter period of the war. (Yorkshire Air Museum)

would lose his life during a raid against Berlin nearly two years later while serving as the station commander of the Pathfinder base at Graveley.

It was not long into 1942 before the first of Croft's new four-engine Halifaxes arrived and from March to June the squadron converted to the new type. When Bomber Command launched its first Thousand Bomber raid against Cologne at the end of May, 78 Squadron was able to contribute twenty-two Halifaxes to the force. Just days later, and with its conversion to the Halifax complete, the squadron moved back to Middleton St George.

Croft was about to be handed over to the Canadians and exactly a year after the airfield opened, the first Wellingtons of 419 (Moose) Squadron RCAF moved into Croft. It had been an unsettling few months for the much travelled crews of 419. Croft was to be their fourth home since the squadron formed just nine months before. Even now, bags could not be unpacked for long as in just a few weeks they would be off again, this time to Middleton St George following the squadron's conversion to the Halifax.

419 Squadron's departure had left room at Croft for a new squadron to form. This was another Canadian squadron, 427 (Lion) Squadron RCAF, which officially formed at Croft on 7 November 1942 from a nucleus of 419. Equipped with Wellington IIIs, the new arrivals flew their first operations from Croft on the night of 14/15 December when three of the squadron's aircraft were part of a force of eighteen Wellingtons sent on minelaying operations to Texel, Heligoland and the Frisians. The squadron's three aircraft were amongst those that went to the Frisians; all returned safely, as did the other Wellingtons involved that night.

Now home to the Canadians, Croft was transferred to 6 (RCAF) Group on its official formation on 1 January 1943. 427 Squadron flew its first bombing op on the night of 15/16 January when six of its aircraft were part of a force of more than 150 aircraft sent to attack the French Atlantic port of Lorient. The Germans were using the port for its U-boats, which had been hassling Allied convoys in the Atlantic. It was Bomber Command's eighth raid against the port but only 6 (RCAF) Group's second bombing operation of the war; the first having taken place against the same target the previous night. One of 427's aircraft failed to return. It was the only Wellington lost that night.

As part of the RAF's re-organization of airfields during 1943, Croft became a sub-station of 64 Base, headquartered at Middleton St George. Gradually the Wellington IIIs were replaced by Wellington Xs, a slightly smaller design with a fuselage structure of light alloy rather than steel. Nearly 4,000 Mark Xs were eventually built, making it the most widely produced Wellington variant of the war.

427 Squadron was led during this period by Wing Commander Dudley Burnside, a 31-year-old former territorial soldier and pre-war RAF pilot from Essex. Burnside had taken command of 427 at the end of 1942 and now led the squadron during the difficult early days of what would become known as the Battle of the Ruhr. On the night of 5/6 March 1943 he was leading the squadron on the opening night of the new campaign. The target was Essen and a mixed force of 442 aircraft was sent to the target, but before Burnside could reach the target his aircraft was hit by flak; killing the navigator and wounding his wireless operator, Flight Sergeant Geoffrey Keen, who was at that time in the astrodome. Despite his wounds Keen returned to his station and for the next two hours he would labour to repair damaged equipment. He also dragged himself to the navigator's position to offer valuable navigational assistance to his captain.

Having been hit by flak, fumes had filled the cockpit and the Wellington had become difficult to control, but Burnside decided to press on to complete the attack. Then, on the way home, enemy night fighters had appeared but with great skill Burnside managed to shake off the attackers and recover the badly damaged bomber back across the North Sea to make an emergency landing in Suffolk. For his skill and courage that night Burnside was awarded a Bar to the DFC he had won earlier in the war. Two of his crew also received the DFC, while Geoffrey Keen was recommended for the Victoria Cross, although he was subsequently awarded the CGM to add to his DFM awarded earlier in the war.

By now, 427 Squadron's time at Croft was nearly up and by the beginning of May 1943 it had moved to Leeming where it would convert to the Halifax. Just days after 427 Squadron moved out, Croft's role changed briefly when it became home to 1664 HCU, equipped with Halifax Vs and responsible for the conversion of bomber crews to the four-engine Halifax.

Although the airfield was now non-operational there were still casualties as training accidents resulted in high losses. Many of these accidents occurred well away from the airfield during training, particularly in bad weather when carrying out training flying around the nearby Moors. Accidents were also quite regular around the airfield's circuit due to the inexperience of the crews.

By the end of 1943 Croft's brief period as a training airfield was over when the HCU moved to Dishforth to be replaced by 431 (Iroquois) Squadron RCAF, which moved in from Tholthorpe during December. The new arrivals had only just resumed operations a few weeks before having replaced its Wellingtons with Halifax Vs. The following day, a second squadron arrived. This was 434 (Bluenose) Squadron RCAF, also equipped with Halifax Vs, which had followed 431 from Tholthorpe to their new home at Croft.

Both these Canadian squadrons would remain at Croft for the rest of the war. Unsurprisingly, their operational pattern would be a similar one. They had arrived at a time when the Battle of Berlin was reaching its climax and the Luftwaffe's night fighter force was at its peak. Both squadrons were involved in what turned out to be Croft's worst night of the war when eight of the base's twenty-eight aircraft taking part in a raid against Berlin on the night of 28/29 January 1944 failed to return; five from 434 and three from 431 Squadron. It was the second raid against the Nazi capital in consecutive nights. Another would be flown just two nights later but it was the raid on 28/29 January that had been the costliest of the three. Bomber Command lost forty-six aircraft that night, including twenty-six Halifaxes from the 241 involved, including the eight from Croft.

By May 1944, both squadrons had re-equipped with the Halifax III and both were to play a part in softening up the enemy defences immediately prior to D-Day, and then afterwards while supporting the Allied breakout from the Normandy beachhead, and by early 1945 both squadrons had exchanged their Halifaxes for Lancasters.

Just as it seemed the war was drawing to an end, Croft received an unwelcome visitor. It was the early hours of 4 March 1945 and the unwelcome visitor was a German Ju 88G, part of a large intruder force that had crossed the North Sea as part of the

Luftwaffe's Operation *Gisela*. Croft's Halifaxes were returning from a raid against the synthetic oil refinery at Bergkamen but one was attacked while in the circuit. It was forced to overshoot the runway and came down in flames in a small wood. Fortunately, the crew survived.

Croft's two squadrons flew their last missions of the war on 25 April 1945 when thirty aircraft, fifteen from each squadron, took part in Bomber Command's raid against the gun batteries on the Frisian island of Wangerooge; two aircraft from 431 Squadron failed to return. The Halifaxes of 434 Squadron then took part in Operation *Exodus*, the repatriation of prisoners of war from Europe.

With the war still raging in the Far East, the two squadrons were allocated to Tiger Force. They left Croft in June and returned to Canada in preparation for moving out to the Pacific but were never deployed. The Japanese surrender meant both squadrons were disbanded instead.

Between December 1943 and June 1945, 431 (Iroquois) Squadron flew 2,573 operational sorties and dropped 14,000 tons of bombs for the loss of seventy-two aircraft and 490 men killed. During the same period, 434 (Bluenose) Squadron flew 2,597 sorties, dropping 10,358 tons of bombs and 225 mines. It had suffered similarly to 431 – seventy-four aircraft lost with the loss of 493 lives.

The former wartime airfield is now home to the Croft Circuit. The section of track shown here is part of a secondary runway that ran almost north–south. (Author)

With the Canadians gone, Croft was used briefly by Mosquitos based at nearby Middleton St George, but with no further use for the airfield in the post-war RAF, Croft then closed. It was then developed as a leading motor racing circuit. Some form of motorsport had taken place at Croft since the late 1920s and with the Second World War over the Darlington and District Motor Club re-formed. Being the only racing circuit in the north-east of England, Croft enjoyed a great deal of success, although the wartime history of this former airfield was not forgotten. For many years the main attraction was the Battle of Britain Meeting, organized by the DDMC in conjunction with the local branch of the RAF Association.

This former wartime bomber airfield is now home to the Croft Circuit and can be found five miles to the south of Darlington. When heading south on the A167 Northallerton Road, turn right into West Lane opposite the turn-off for the village of Dalton-on-Tees. West Lane takes you down to the former airfield. The racing circuit is on the eastern part of the former airfield. Part of one of the secondary runways, which was aligned near north–south, and part of the former perimeter track now make up part of the circuit. The circuit also heads north-west along what was the other secondary runway.

Part of the former main runway at Croft is now the paddock. A grass strip running parallel to the runway is still used by light aircraft for private flying. (Author)

A section of the former main runway, which ran in a near east–west direction, is now the paddock and a grass strip running parallel to the runway is still used by light aircraft for private flying. The old air traffic control tower lay derelict for many years but is no longer there, although its foundations can still be seen on the eastern side of what is now the racing circuit near one of the old wartime brick buildings. On the wall of one of the main buildings at the entrance to the circuit is a plaque in memory of those airmen and aircrews who served at Croft between 1941 and 1945 under 4 Group and 6 (RCAF) Group of Bomber Command; the plaque shows the squadrons, aircraft types and dates served.

Although there is general public access to the Croft Circuit, gaining access to its far side and to other parts of the former airfield requires prior permission. The original entrance to the airfield was from West Lane. When travelling down the lane from the main road, instead of turning right to the Croft Circuit, continue southwards along West Lane for around 400 yards and the original entrance was on the right. It is now a private farm. A gun emplacement and shelter have survived, although the land is private and these cannot be seen from the lane.

In addition to the Croft Circuit, a memorial of a bronze statue of an airman stands on the south-eastern corner of the village of

A bronze statue of an airman stands on the south-eastern corner of the village of Dalton-on-Tees to honour those who served at Croft during the Second World War. (Author)

Dalton-on-Tees. It can be found at the entrance to the village from the main A167 Northallerton Road and stands in memory of, and to honour those, who served at Croft during the Second World War. It was erected in 1987 and unveiled by Brigadier-General Bill Newson RCAF and dedicated by the Very Reverend John Southgate, Dean of York, to the members of 431 (Iroquois) and 434 (Bluenose) RCAF Squadrons. Next to the memorial is a plaque summarizing the wartime history of the two Canadian squadrons.

Summary of units based at Croft during the Second World War

78 Squadron (EY) – 20 Oct 41 (Middleton St George) – 10 Jun 42 (Middleton St George)
Whitley V (Oct 41 – Mar 42)
Halifax II (Mar – Jun 42)

419 (Moose) Squadron RCAF (VR) – 30 Sep 42 (Topcliffe) – 8 Nov 42 (Middleton St George)
Wellington I/III

427 (Lion) Squadron RCAF (ZL) – 7 Nov 42 (Formed) – 3 May 43 (Leeming)
Wellington III (Nov 42 – Apr 43)
Wellington X (Feb – May 43)

1664 HCU – 10 May 43 (Formed) – 7 Dec 43 (Dishforth)
Halifax V

431 (Iroquois) Squadron RCAF (SE) – 10 Dec 43 (Tholthorpe) – 12 Jun 45 (Disbanded)
Halifax V (Dec 43 – Apr 44)
Halifax III (Mar – Oct 44)
Lancaster X (Oct 44 – Jun 45)

434 (Bluenose) Squadron RCAF (WL) – 11 Dec 43 (Tholthorpe) – 15 Jun 45 (Disbanded)
Halifax V (Dec 43 – May 44)
Halifax III (May – Dec 44)
Lancaster X (Dec 44 – Jun 45)
Lancaster I (Feb – Mar 45)

Chapter 20

Dalton

Location – North Yorkshire, six miles north-east of Ripon. Status – Satellite airfield. 61 (RCAF) Base – sub-station of Topcliffe.

Another of Yorkshire's wartime bomber airfields is Dalton, which takes its name from the village nearby. Situated just to the south of Topcliffe airfield, Dalton opened in November 1941 as its satellite. Dalton's first residents were Whitleys of 102 Squadron, which arrived from Topcliffe the same month. The squadron flew its first operations from its new home at the end of the month when seven aircraft took part in a small-scale raid on Emden; one failed to return.

At that time, Dalton was far from complete and it would be another year before the airfield was brought up to full Bomber Command standard. Nonetheless, it was considered ready enough and suitable for the operation of new four-engine heavy bombers and so the following month the first Halifaxes started to arrive.

The squadron immediately formed a conversion flight for its crews to be trained on the new type and flew its final Whitley operations on the last night of January 1942. But because of the amount of time it took to convert to the Halifax, not helped by the aircraft suffering technical problems along the way, it would be more than two months before operations resumed from the airfield. However, at the beginning of June, after taking part in two consecutive raids against Essen, one being the second of Bomber Command's Thousand Bomber raids, the squadron moved back to Topcliffe. Unfortunately, though, 102 Squadron left Dalton on a bit of a down having lost five aircraft during its last two raids.

A Whitley of 102 Squadron. The squadron moved to Dalton in late 1941 but soon began converting to the Halifax. (Peter Green via Ken Delve)

With 102 Squadron gone, Halifaxes of 76 and 78 Conversion Flights arrived the following month but moved out again just weeks later to become part of 1652 HCU at Marston Moor. Dalton now went through a period of major reconstruction. The airfield had been earmarked for the Canadians and so it was brought up to Class A standard with three concrete runways. The main runway, 1,800 yards long, was aligned just off east–west, while its two subsidiaries, one running from the north-east to the south-west and the other almost north–south, were 1,500 yards and 1,400 yards respectively.

With accommodation for around 1,300 personnel, Dalton was not one of Bomber Command's biggest bases but the airfield re-opened in November 1942 in time for the arrival of the Wellingtons of the newly formed 428 (Ghost) Squadron RCAF of 4 Group. Almost immediately, though, Dalton was transferred to the all-Canadian 6 (RCAF) Group on its formation at the beginning of 1943.

Operations under its new chain of command began on the night of 26/27 January when six Wellingtons joined a force of more than 150 aircraft to carry out an attack against the U-boat base at the French port of Lorient; all of the squadron's aircraft returned safely.

Under the RAF's re-organization of airfields during 1943, Dalton became a sub-station of 61 Base, headquartered at

Topcliffe. It was then briefly home to Wellingtons of 424 (Tiger) Squadron RCAF, which arrived from Leeming in early May but the Tigers only stayed a matter of days as they were on their way to North Africa. However, with the desert war all but over the squadron would return to Yorkshire later in the year. But just three weeks after the Tigers had left Dalton, 428 Squadron was also on its way. The squadron left for Middleton St George in early June to convert to the Halifax and so ended Dalton's role as an operational base.

Dalton now took on a training role. A new heavy conversion unit, 1666 HCU, had already formed a few weeks before with its ageing Halifaxes to train and prepare crews for their frontline operational tours. The HCU was then joined at Dalton by another training unit, 1691 (Bomber) Gunnery Training Flight, later to be renamed 1695 Bomber Defence Training Flight (BDTF), with the task of training air gunners. But by October the HCU had moved to Wombleton, leaving the BDTF as the airfield's only resident flying unit.

At the end of the year Dalton was briefly home to the Canadians of 420 (Snowy Owl) Squadron RCAF. The Snowy Owls had returned from North Africa, having carried out raids against Italian ports and airfields. With the Allies now advancing through Italy, the squadron was no longer required in the Mediterranean. Leaving its Wellingtons behind, the Snowy Owls had returned to the UK by sea, staying briefly at

This Halifax of 102 Squadron would require some repairs before being ready for operations again, having swung off the runway on landing at Dalton. (IWM)

The site of the former airfield of Dalton can be seen from Eldmire Lane, which runs along what was its western boundary down to an industrial estate that has now spread across the southern part of the airfield. (Author)

Dalton before converting to the Halifax III and moving on to Tholthorpe.

As the war entered its final phase, Dalton was transferred to 7 (Training) Group but it would retain its link with 6 (RCAF) Group by training Canadian personnel for the rest of the war. From the summer of 1944 it was home to 6 (RCAF) Group Aircrew School, a holding unit for aircrew between their training with the OTUs and the HCUs. This did not involve flying but the syllabus for the student crews included physical training as well as lectures on survival and escape and evasion. At the end of the war the BDTF and Aircrew School disbanded, and by the end of 1945 the airfield had closed, after which most of the land reverted to agriculture.

This former wartime airfield can be found six miles to the north-east of Ripon, between the villages of Topcliffe and Dalton; it is actually nearer to the village of Topcliffe than RAF Topcliffe. To find the site of Dalton, take the A167 Long Street eastwards from the village of Topcliffe. Soon after passing under the main A168 there is a turning right into Dalton Lane. Follow the lane for about 300 yards to another turn-off right. This is Eldmire Lane, which marks the north-western corner of the former airfield. The lane runs southwards along its western boundary down to an industrial estate, which has now spread across the entire area of what was once the southern part of the airfield and where many former wartime buildings have been taken over as business premises. Continuing along Dalton Lane takes you along the airfield's northern boundary, with the village of Dalton marking the north-eastern corner.

Summary of units based at Dalton during the Second World War

102 Squadron (DY) – 15 Nov 41 (Topcliffe) – 7 Jun 42 (Topcliffe)
Whitley V (Nov 41 – Feb 42)
Halifax II (Dec 41 – Jun 42)

1652 HCU – Jun – Jul 42
Halifax I

428 (Ghost) Squadron RCAF (NA) – 7 Nov 42 (Formed) – 4 Jun 43 (Middleton St George)
Wellington III (Nov 42 – May 43)
Wellington X (Dec 42 – Jun 43)

424 (Tiger) Squadron RCAF (QB) – 3 May 43 (Leeming) – 15 May 43 (North Africa)
Wellington X

1666 HCU – May 43 (Formed) – Oct 43 (Wombleton)
Halifax I

420 (Snowy Owl) Squadron RCAF (PT) – 6 Nov 43 (North Africa) – 12 Dec 43 (Tholthorpe)
Halifax III

CHAPTER 21

Dishforth (Ripon)

Location – North Yorkshire, four miles east of Ripon.
Status – Operational airfield. 63 (RCAF) Base – sub-station of Leeming, after which it became a training airfield and part of 61 (RCAF) Base, headquartered by Topcliffe.

One of Yorkshire's pre-Second World War airfields is Dishforth, which takes its name from the nearby village. It was during the RAF's expansion of the mid-1930s that a site was surveyed to the south of the village and just on the eastern side of the A1 (although the airfield would eventually expand across the Great North Road to its western side). The land was considered suitable for development as a bomber airfield and so work soon began.

Dishforth opened in September 1936 as part of 3 Group, Bomber Command. It was the second of Yorkshire's five pre-war bomber airfields to open (Driffield being the first), and because of its well-constructed and permanent facilities, Dishforth would become a popular posting for wartime personnel. By early 1937, the airfield was home to two squadrons, 10 and 78 Squadrons. Both were equipped with Handley Page Heyfords, a twin-engine biplane bomber and an important part of the RAF's inventory of the 1930s, but the Heyford was to be the last biplane bomber to enter service and so would have a relatively short service life. By the end of the year the squadrons had replaced them with the Whitley.

By the outbreak of the Second World War, both units were still at Dishforth, now one of Bomber Command's main airfields of 4 Group. While 78 Squadron was used as a feeder squadron for new crews arriving with squadrons of 4 Group, the Whitleys of 10 Squadron took part in leaflet dropping over Germany.

10 Squadron was then under the command of Wing Commander William 'Bull' Staton, a former First World War fighter ace with twenty-six victories. For now, the Nickelling sorties went on, with the monotony of leaflet dropping only being broken during the occasional moonlit nights when the crews were tasked with carrying out visual reconnaissance of specific areas of Germany. And it was during one of these sorties, on the night of 1/2 October 1939, that a Whitley of 10 Squadron flew over Berlin. It was the first Bomber Command aircraft to do so.

By the end of the year, 78 Squadron had moved to Linton-on-Ouse, exchanging bases with 51 Squadron, and it would be the Whitleys of 10 and 51 Squadrons that would operate together from Dishforth for the next few months. The winter weather made Nickelling sorties difficult and extremely uncomfortable for the crew. The temperature inside the aircraft fell to –20 degrees centigrade with the crew having to endure hours in freezing cold conditions with no heating and no way of alleviating the problem, other than bashing the extremities of the body to try and create some heat. The poor rear gunner, in particular, cramped in his rear turret and almost open to the elements, suffered most of all.

It was still the period of the so-called Phoney War and the bombing of mainland Germany remained prohibited, but the night of 19/20 March 1940 marked an early but important raid for Bomber Command following the German attack on the Royal Navy at Scapa Flow. Bomber Command had been ordered to carry out a reprisal attack with the chosen target being the German seaplane base at Hörnum on the southernmost tip of the island of Sylt, and well away from civilian areas. Twenty Hampdens and thirty Whitleys, including eight from Dishforth led by Staton, took part in what was Bomber Command's largest raid of the war to date. The Whitleys attacked first, dropping their bomb loads of 1,500 lb, followed by the Hampdens. Altogether, more than 20 tons of high explosives and a thousand incendiary bombs were dropped, although a post-raid reconnaissance could not be carried out until the following month, making it all but impossible to assess whether the raid had been a success or not. One of Dishforth's aircraft was lost, that flown by Flight Lieutenant John Baskerville, a 25-year-old Canadian serving with 51 Squadron.

It had now been more than six months since Britain's declaration of war, yet this raid marked the RAF's first real bombing operation of the war and was the first time RAF bombers dropped bombs on a land target. When Italy entered the war in June 1940, Dishforth's crews made up part of a force of thirty-six Whitleys tasked with carrying out the RAF's first bombing raid against an Italian target of the war. The Whitleys first flew to the Channel Islands to refuel before making the long trip across France and the Alps to bomb factories in Turin. But bad weather encountered over the Alps prevented most of the Whitleys from reaching Turin and in the end only nine aircraft managed to arrive in the target area, although the designated factories could not be identified and so seven bombed railway yards whilst the other two bombed Genoa instead.

10 Squadron moved to Leeming in July to be replaced by 78 Squadron, now returning to Dishforth from Linton-on-Ouse. The crews of 78 were in action almost immediately, flying their first operations within days of their return. The Whitley was a versatile aircraft and because it had been designed with a ventral turret, it was possible to have the turret removed to create an exit hole for the dropping of men and supplies. In early February 1941, 24-year-old Flight Lieutenant James 'Willie' Tait, an experienced pre-war pilot from Manchester and now serving with 51 Squadron, led four aircraft from each of Dishforth's two squadrons to Malta in preparation for what was then considered a rather unusual mission.

What followed was Operation *Colossus*, the first British airborne drop of military forces. On 10 February 1941, thirty-eight paratroopers belonging to a specially formed unit called X Troop were dropped by the Whitleys in southern Italy to destroy a fresh water aqueduct near Calitri. It was hoped the destruction of the aqueduct would hamper Italian military efforts in the region. But the raid was carried out with only moderate success, although it did mark the first British airborne operation of the war. For his leadership, Tait was awarded the DSO and given temporary promotion to the rank of squadron leader. He then left Dishforth to join 35 Squadron at Linton-on-Ouse, the first squadron to be equipped with the new four-engine Halifax heavy bomber.

78 Squadron moved to Middleton St George in April 1941, leaving 51 Squadron to operate alone from Dishforth for another year. During this time the Whitleys were joined by Airspeed Oxfords of 12 Beam Approach Training Flight, later re-numbered 1512 BATF.

In the absence of any long-range transport aircraft for dropping supplies or paratroopers, the Whitley continued to be used in many guises. *Colossus* had tested the concept of an airborne assault and was considered successful enough to expand British airborne forces. In February 1942, Dishforth's Whitleys were again to be used for an airborne assault, this time against a German *Würzburg* radar installation at Bruneval on the north coast of France.

The plan to capture an enemy radar site at night, and then dismantle it so that parts could be taken back to Britain for expert evaluation, would make the raid on Bruneval one of the most audacious of the Second World War. Given the codename Operation *Biting*, the RAF element of the mission was given to 51 Squadron, now under the command of Wing Commander Charles 'Pick' Pickard DSO DFC, a well-known public figure following his starring role in the 1941 wartime propaganda film *Target for Tonight* in which he featured as a Wellington pilot of *F for Freddie*.

There was little time for much training. The operation needed to be complete by the end of February due to the combination of the moon, a rising tide and the general weather conditions, and so the Whitley crews flew down to Thruxton in Hampshire for the final stages of training, which included a practice para drop on Salisbury Plain.

Late in the evening of 27 February twelve Whitleys took off for the raid with each aircraft carrying ten men and equipment. Diversionary air raids had been planned for the night to keep the Luftwaffe and anti-aircraft flak batteries occupied and these were already in full operation. The Whitleys crossed the Channel at low level to avoid being detected by enemy radar. As they approached the French coastline at around 1,500 feet the clear visibility made navigation relatively easy. They initially paralleled the French coastline towards Le Havre and then turned left on a north-easterly heading towards Bruneval. Then, dropping down to below 500 feet, they made their final run-in towards their drop zones. With Pickard leading, it was just after midnight when the drops took place.

The raid that followed proved to be a success and was given great coverage by the media. For his leadership of the drop Pickard received a Bar to his DSO. The success of the raid not only ensured the expansion of British airborne forces but it was the technical knowledge gained by British scientists that was the most important aspect of the raid. Examination of the *Würzburg* equipment showed the radar to be vulnerable to new jamming techniques under consideration at the time and this led to the development of *Window*, aluminium strips dropped in bundles and used as an effective countermeasure against German radars during the latter half of the war – a development that would save countless lives amongst the crews of Bomber Command.

51 Squadron proved a versatile squadron and also supported the daring naval raid on St Nazaire at the end of March. Then, in May 1942, 51 Squadron was loaned to Coastal Command to help counter the growing threat of the German U-boats in the Atlantic, bringing an end to its days at Dishforth.

Dishforth now prepared for the arrival of the Canadians and the first unit to form was 425 (Alouette) Squadron RCAF, which formed in June with Wellington IIIs under the command of Wing Commander Joe St Pierre. The squadron flew its first operations on the night of 5/6 October when eight of its Wellingtons made up part of a force of more than 250 aircraft sent to attack the town of Aachen. However, bad weather meant the raid was not a success. One of the squadron's Wellingtons crashed on its way to the target while two others had to return early having encountered severe icing. More bad weather over Germany meant that only one of the squadron's aircraft managed to find the target.

As 4 Group continued to expand, a second Canadian Wellington squadron formed at Dishforth. This was 426 (Thunderbird) Squadron RCAF under the command of 31-year-old Wing Commander Sedley Blanchard from Brandon in Manitoba. Blanchard was a former Canadian Army officer but had resigned his commission to join the RCAF before the war. After a number of postings in Canada he had flown to England in the summer of 1942 and after training on the Wellington had arrived at Dishforth to take command of the new squadron.

With the formation of 6 (RCAF) Group on 1 January 1943, Dishforth and its squadrons were transferred to the new all-Canadian group. The airfield also became home to the group's communications flight and when the RAF re-organized its airfields into a base system, Dishforth became a sub-station of 63 Base, headquartered at Leeming.

6 (RCAF) Group's first operational loss occurred during its debut bombing raid against Lorient on 14/15 January. Unfortunately, the aircraft lost that night was one of Dishforth's Wellingtons, BK165 of 426 Squadron, flown by 21-year-old Pilot Officer George Milne from Calgary in Alberta. All the crew (five Canadians and one from England) were killed when the aircraft came down in the sea. It was one of seven aircraft from the squadron taking part in the raid.

The following month, 426 Squadron and Dishforth suffered a notable loss when Sedley Blanchard failed to return from a raid against Cologne on the night of 14/15 February. His aircraft had been attacked by a night fighter while on its way back from the target and came down near the Dutch town of Beegden. The bodies of the crew were recovered and are now buried in the Jonkerbos War Cemetery in Holland.

Wing Commander Leslie Crooks DSO DFC commanded the Thunderbirds of 426 Squadron RCAF at Dishforth from early 1943. It was his second operational tour but Crooks was soon to lose his life when he failed to return from a raid against the German V-weapons research establishment at Peenemünde on the night of 17/18 August 1943. (AHB)

Command of the squadron now passed to 33-year-old Wing Commander Leslie Crooks DFC. Crooks was not a Canadian. He had been born in Bishop Auckland and joined the RAF as an apprentice at the age of seventeen. He had then become a sergeant pilot and served in Iraq during the inter-war years but more recently had settled in Peterborough with his wife. His DFC had been awarded two years earlier while serving as a Whitley pilot with 58 Squadron at Linton-on-Ouse, and this was to be his second operational tour.

Crooks would lead by example and was soon awarded the DSO following a raid against Duisburg on the night of 26/27 April. While approaching the target his aircraft was raked by cannon shells from an enemy night fighter. He immediately threw the Wellington into a corkscrew manoeuvre to evade the attacker, but his aircraft had already sustained much damage. Although one aileron and half the port tail plane had been shot away, and the hydraulic and electrical systems were rendered inoperative, Crooks managed to nurse the crippled bomber back home. However, it was not possible to effect a safe landing and so the crew were left with no option other than to abandon their aircraft. They all landed safely and soon after came the announcement of the DSO for Crooks, his citation concluding:

> *In the face of heavy odds, Wing Commander Crooks set an example worthy of high praise.*

426 Squadron moved to Linton-on-Ouse in June but Leslie Crooks would lose his life on his eighth op with the squadron during Bomber Command's raid against the German V-weapons research establishment at Peenemünde on the night of 17/18 August 1943. 426 had followed 425 Squadron out of Dishforth, after the latter had left for North Africa the month before, although it would briefly return at the end of the year to re-join 6 (RCAF) Group prior to moving to Tholthorpe to re-equip with the Halifax. The Oxfords of the BATF had also moved out.

These departures were all planned as Dishforth was about to undergo major construction work to bring the airfield up to the standard bomber design in preparation for the arrival of four-engine heavy bombers. The improvements included three hardened runways, the main one being nearly 2,000 yards long and running just off north–south, parallel to the A1, with the two intersecting runways, both nearly 1,400 yards long, aligned near east–west and north-east to south-west. A hardened perimeter track connected thirty-six aircraft dispersals with the runways, with five hangars and the main technical site all situated on the eastern part of the airfield.

Dishforth re-opened in November 1943 but its operational days were over and the airfield instead took on a training role. Within days the Halifaxes of 1664 HCU moved in from Croft and for the following year the HCU was the only resident unit. Dishforth was now operating as part of 61 (RCAF) Base, headquartered by Topcliffe and with other sub-stations at Dalton and Wombleton, with responsibility for the training of new bomber crews for the squadrons of 6 (RCAF) Group. But like other Bomber Command training units the HCU had its share of accidents and casualties. It was still operating old Halifax IIs and a few Mark Vs and in one month alone, October 1944, six aircraft were lost during training with the loss of more than twenty lives.

During the last months of the war 1695 Bomber Defence Training Flight moved to Dishforth, although by the end of hostilities both the BDTF and the HCU had been disbanded. With the war over and its flying units gone, a number of the airfield's

In the village of Dishforth is a sundial on a stone plinth, erected by the villagers in gratitude to all those who served at the airfield during the Second World War. (Author)

Nissen huts were used for the temporary accommodation of German prisoners of war before they were returned home.

Dishforth was then transferred to Transport Command and used in the training role until 1961 when the airfield was placed on care and maintenance. However, it was never fully disposed of and was used by the RAF as a relief landing ground for training aircraft based in the Vale of York. In the early 1990s, Dishforth was transferred to the army and became home to helicopters. In May 2016 the Army Air Corps flew from the airfield for the last time to be replaced by a unit of the Royal Logistic Corps. It brought to an end twenty-five years of army flying from Dishforth and marked the end of an era of army aviation in Yorkshire and the north of England.

Being a military base, entrance is by prior permission only. It is four miles to the east of Ripon and just half a mile south of the village of Dishforth, adjacent to the A1M Great North Road. This road, and the A168 that runs on the west side of the A1M, runs parallel with the airfield's western boundary. In the village of Dishforth, outside the village hall, is a sundial on a stone plinth. It was erected by the villagers and dedicated in 1991 in gratitude to all those who served with the Royal Canadian Air Force at Dishforth between 1942 and 1945.

Summary of units based at Dishforth during the Second World War

10 Squadron (ZA) – 1937 – 8 Jul 40 (Leeming)
Whitley IV/V

78 Squadron (EY) – 1937 – 14 Oct 39 (Linton-on-Ouse)
Whitley I/IV

51 Squadron (MH) – 9 Dec 39 (Linton-on-Ouse) – 5 May 42 (Chivenor)
Whitley IV/V

78 Squadron (EY) – 15 Jul 40 (Linton-on-Ouse) – 6 Apr 41 (Middleton St George)
Whitley V

425 (Alouette) Squadron RCAF (KW) – 25 Jun 42 (Formed) – 15 May 43 (North Africa)
Wellington III

426 (Thunderbird) Squadron RCAF (OW) – 15 Oct 42 (Formed) – 17 Jun 43 (Linton-on-Ouse)
Wellington III/X

425 (Alouette) Squadron RCAF (KW) – 6 Nov 43 (North Africa) – 11 Dec 43 (Tholthorpe)
No aircraft

1664 HCU – Dec 43 – Apr 45
Halifax V/III

Chapter 22

East Moor

Location – North Yorkshire, seven miles north of York.
Status – Operational airfield. 62 (RCAF) Base – sub-station of Linton-on-Ouse.

One of Yorkshire's later airfields to have been developed as part of Bomber Command's expansion during the Second World War, East Moor did not open until June 1942. Initially allocated to 4 Group, East Moor had taken its name from the land where it was built and was constructed to the standard three hardened runways design with the main runway, 1,900 yards long, running in an almost north–south direction from the village of Sutton-on-the-Forest. Thirty-six aircraft dispersals were mostly constructed on the eastern side of the airfield, three hangars were built for maintenance and there was enough temporary accommodation for 2,500 personnel.

The airfield's first residents were the Halifaxes of 158 Squadron, which arrived from Driffield the same month. The squadron was still in the process of converting to its new four-engine bomber from the Wellington and so 158 was effectively non-operational when it arrived. It had, however, provided eleven aircraft for Bomber Command's all-out effort against Cologne on the last night of May in the first of the so-called Thousand Bomber raids; all of the squadron's aircraft had returned safely.

With Harris ordering another all-out effort, against Bremen on the night of 25/26 June, in what was the third of the Thousand Bomber raids, 158 Squadron again took part. One of its aircraft, flown by 21-year-old Pilot Officer Les Bradbury, failed to return. However, Bradbury managed to successfully ditch in the North Sea after running out of fuel. Sadly, though, his crew were to

A Halifax of 432 (Leaside) Squadron RCAF lands at East Moor. The squadron arrived in September 1943 and remained until the end of the war. (AHB)

be less fortunate just a matter of a few weeks later when they became East Moor's first casualties over Germany.

The Bremen raid had been East Moor's first experience of operations and during the next four months 158 Squadron took part in most of Bomber Command's major efforts, losing sixteen aircraft along the way. However, the squadron's stay at East Moor was soon over as it left for Rufforth in early November 1942. East Moor was one of a number of Yorkshire airfields earmarked for the new Canadian bomber group about to form.

With 158 Squadron gone, East Moor then became home to 429 (Bison) Squadron RCAF, which formed just days later. The new squadron was initially allocated to 4 Group but this was only for administrative purposes until the formation of 6 (RCAF) Group became official.

The Canadians flew their first operational sorties on the night of 21/22 January 1943 when four aircraft took part in minelaying off the Frisian Islands. One aircraft, flown by Flying Officer Ian Johnson, a New Zealander, failed to return. His Wellington is believed to have been shot down by flak over the Dutch coast. The young navigator, 20-year-old Sergeant Charles Risingham, was a local Yorkshire lad. In contrast, the crew's bomb aimer, Flying Officer Ian Stirton from the Isle of Wight, was aged forty-one and sadly became one of Bomber Command's oldest casualties of the war. Five nights later the squadron took part in its first bombing operation of the war when ten of its Wellingtons were part of a force of more than 150 aircraft sent to attack the French Atlantic port of Lorient. One of the squadron's aircraft failed to return and amongst the crew was 17-year-old Sergeant Desmond Lewis, one of Bomber Command's youngest casualties of the war.

The transfer of East Moor and its squadron to the newly formed 6 (RCAF) Group officially occurred in April and under the RAF's reorganization of its airfields to a base system, East Moor became a sub-station of 62 (RCAF) Base with its headquarters at Linton-on-Ouse.

At the beginning of June command of 429 Squadron passed from Wing Commander J Owen, the squadron's first CO, to Joe Savard, a remarkable young Canadian pilot with a DFC. Savard was then Bomber Command's youngest CO at the age of just twenty-two but sadly his life would soon be cut short during a raid against Mülheim on the night of 22/23 June. And so, the squadron now picked up another CO. This was Wing Commander James Piddington, also with a DFC, who took command at the end of June 1943. But Piddington was also soon to lose his life. He was killed on the night of 27/28 July during the Battle of Hamburg when his Wellington was shot down by a night fighter over the target. It was the only Wellington lost that night.

Piddington's successor, Wing Commander 'JD' Pattison, was 429 Squadron's fourth CO in just over two months. The squadron had now been joined at East Moor by 1679 HCU, which had formed at the end of May, with responsibility for training new crews for the Lancaster squadrons of 6 (RCAF) Group. As the Canadian group continued to expand, changes were made along the way and amongst these was the departure of 429 Squadron to Leeming to be replaced by 432 (Leaside) Squadron RCAF, which would remain at East Moor for the rest of the war.

One unfortunate fact associated with East Moor involved the loss of a Wellington of 432 Squadron. The aircraft was LN451 'QO-W', flown by Warrant Officer Douglas Baker, which was lost during a raid against Hannover on the night of 8/9 October 1943. 432 was one of just two Wellington squadrons taking part that night and had put up fourteen of the twenty-six aircraft taking part. The rest of the large force of more than 500 aircraft was made up of four-engine heavies, Lancasters and Halifaxes, and it was the night that marked the last Bomber Command raid involving the Wellington, making 'QO-W' the last Wellington to have been lost on bombing operations.

Having replaced its Wellingtons with the Lancaster II (powered by Bristol Hercules engines rather than Rolls-Royce Merlins), 432 Squadron flew its first operations with its new type on the night of 26/27 November 1943 when ten aircraft were part of an all-Lancaster force of 450 aircraft sent to attack Berlin. It was Bomber Command's third raid against the Nazi capital in just five nights in what was the opening phase of the Battle of Berlin. The Lancasters dropped more than 1,500 tons of bombs that night for the loss of twenty-eight aircraft, although all of 432's aircraft returned safely.

The following month, the HCU moved out to a new airfield at Wombleton, leaving 432 Squadron to operate alone from East Moor. By the time the Battle of Berlin ended in March 1944 the squadron had exchanged its Lancasters for the Halifax III.

In July, the squadron was joined at East Moor by the much-travelled 415 (Swordfish) Squadron RCAF. Unlike most Canadian squadrons, 415 had a varied operational existence, ranging from being a Beaufort torpedo-bomber unit on the south coast of England with Coastal Command to now becoming a Yorkshire-based heavy bomber squadron of Bomber Command. The Halifax was to be 415 Squadron's sixth aircraft type and East Moor its fifth operational base. There had also been several operational detachments elsewhere in between.

415 Squadron flew its first operations in its new role on the night of 28/29 July 1944. Sixteen aircraft made up part of a mixed force of 300-plus Lancasters and Halifaxes sent to Hamburg. Eighteen Halifaxes failed to return, including one from East Moor, an aircraft belonging to 432 Squadron. The war was now into its final year and the two Canadian squadrons continued to operate side-by-side from East Moor with many highs and lows along the way, and amongst the many tragic tales of East Moor's wartime existence was the collision of two Halifaxes from 415 Squadron on 21 August 1944. The collision occurred near Selby while the two aircraft were flying in formation. All fourteen men on board died, including the squadron commander, 25-year-old Wing Commander John McNeill DFC, and one of the flight

commanders, Squadron Leader Brian Wilmot, aged just twenty-one but already a holder of the DFC and Bar.

Both squadrons flew their last missions of the war on 25 April 1945 during Bomber Command's raid against gun batteries on the Frisian island of Wangerooge, when East Moor provided thirty-seven of the 308 Halifaxes taking part; all of East Moor's aircraft returned safely. Within days of the war ending both squadrons were disbanded. There were a few movements in out of the airfield during the following year but East Moor was not part of the RAF's post-war plan. The airfield closed in June 1946 and over the years the land has reverted to agriculture.

The former airfield of East Moor is seven miles north of York and less than a mile to the south-east of the village of Sutton-on-the-Forest, on the eastern side of the B1363 Carr Lane. From the village of Sutton-on-the-Forest follow Carr Lane southwards for less than a mile. This is the north-western corner of the former airfield. Continuing along the lane takes you down the airfield's western boundary and adjacent to where the main runway ran just off to your left. Parts of the runway and perimeter track are still visible. The entrance to the former airfield was off Carr Lane and farm buildings mark where the technical site once stood. In the centre of the village of Sutton-on-the-Forest is a stone pillar

In the centre of the village of Sutton-on-the-Forest is a stone pillar memorial, designed as a sun dial, dedicated to those who served with the three Canadian squadrons at East Moor during the Second World War. (Author)

memorial designed as a sun dial. It was unveiled in 1990 to those who served with the three Canadian squadrons at East Moor during the Second World War. The memorial is on the eastern side of the village at a mini-roundabout where Carr Lane meets Main Street and the B1363 Stillington Road.

Summary of units based at East Moor during the Second World War

158 Squadron (NP) – 4 Jun 42 (Driffield) – 5 Nov 42 (Rufforth)
Halifax II

429 (Bison) Squadron RCAF (AL) – 7 Nov 42 (Formed) – 11 Aug 43 (Leeming)
Wellington III/X

1679 HCU – May 43 – Dec 43
Lancaster II

432 (Leaside) Squadron RCAF (QO) – 18 Sep 43 (Skipton-on-Swale) – 15 May 45 (Disbanded)
Wellington X (Sep – Oct 43)
Lancaster II (Oct 43 – Feb 44)
Halifax III (Feb – Jul 44)
Halifax VII (Jun 44 – May 45)

415 (Swordfish) Squadron RCAF (6U) – 12 Jul 44 (Manston) – 15 May 45 (Disbanded)
Halifax III (Jul 44 – May 45)
Halifax VII (Mar – May 45)

CHAPTER 23

Leeming

Location – North Yorkshire, four miles south-west of Northallerton.
Status – Operational airfield. HQ 63 (RCAF) Base.

One of the best known airfields in the north of England, and still used by the RAF today, is Leeming, one of Yorkshire's, and Bomber Command's, most important airfields of the Second World War.

Identified as one of many sites deemed suitable for development as part of the RAF's preparation for the Second World War, work began in late 1938 close to the village by which the airfield takes its name. The site was something of an obvious one. A flying club had been established on land to the south of Leeming Bar, close to the A1 Great North Road and part of the Duke of Cleveland's estate. The land was taken over by the Air

Whitleys of 10 Squadron pictured at Leeming during the opening stage of the war. (RAF Leeming)

Ministry just before the outbreak of war and turned into a major RAF airfield with three hardened runways (the main runway being nearly 2,000 yards long and aligned almost north–south parallel to the Great North Road), five hangars for maintenance, permanent brick buildings for administrative and technical use, and enough accommodation to eventually house nearly 3,000 personnel.

RAF Leeming opened in June 1940 and like other airfields in North Yorkshire was allocated to 4 Group, Bomber Command. However, its first residents were a detachment of Blenheim fighters of 219 Squadron based at nearby Catterick, although these were to move out later in the year. The first bombers arrived in July. These were Whitleys of 10 Squadron, under the command of its new CO, Wing Commander Sidney Bufton, a former Welsh international hockey player who would later become one of Bomber Command's legendary characters for his work in establishing the Pathfinders.

The first bomber ops from Leeming were flown on the night of 20/21 July 1940 when nine of the squadron's aircraft bombed the Luftwaffe airfield at Wejendorf in Holland, one of a number of raids made by Bomber Command against enemy airfields that night. Two weeks later, 7 Squadron re-formed at Leeming to become Bomber Command's first squadron equipped with the Stirling, the first of the RAF's four-engine bombers to enter service. However, the Stirling was not destined to stay long in Yorkshire and within three months the squadron had moved to Boscombe Down and then to Oakington, part of 3 Group, from where it would fly its first operations with the new type.

Leeming's personnel would get used to seeing units come and go. For example, during the last week of August the airfield was home to a second Whitley squadron, 102 Squadron, which arrived from Driffield but left for Scotland just days later. Then, in November, Leeming was briefly home to the Halifaxes of 35 Squadron. The squadron had re-formed with the task of bringing the Halifax, the second of the new four-engine heavy bombers, into operational service. Once again, Leeming had a key role to play in the build-up to operational readiness of one of the RAF's new four-engine heavy bombers, but by the end of the year 35 Squadron had moved on to Linton-on-Ouse from where it would later commence operations.

For now, the comings and goings were over, and by the end of 1940 only 10 Squadron remained. Leeming was now under the command of Group Captain William Staton. Known to those under his command as 'King Kong' because of his size, Staton had been decorated three times during the First World War (Military Cross, DFC and Bar) and had since added the DSO and Bar for his courage and leadership during the Second World War.

The flamboyant 42-year-old Staton was a legend as the station commander and he would command Leeming until the spring of 1941, after which he was posted to the Far East just months before Japan launched its entry into the war. Staton would later be captured by the Japanese and spend the rest of the war in captivity, often being subjected to ill-treatment for refusing to co-operate under interrogation. Nonetheless, Staton survived his ordeal and remained in the post-war RAF to reach the rank of air vice-marshal. He also became the captain of the British Olympic shooting teams of 1948 and 1952.

Meanwhile, 10 Squadron had continued to operate alone from Leeming until September 1941 when Whitleys of 77 Squadron arrived from Topcliffe. The new arrivals were under the command of another legendary RAF officer, Wing Commander Donald Bennett, later known for commanding the Pathfinders. 77 Squadron was soon in action but suffered its first losses from Leeming on the night of 6/7 September, when three of its Whitleys failed to return from a raid on a chemical factory at Hüls. 10 Squadron had also taken part in the raid with two of its aircraft lost that night. Of the forty-one Whitleys that had taken part in the attack, five were lost; all were from Leeming.

By the end of 1941, 10 Squadron had converted to the Halifax II and carried out its first operation with the type on 18 December with a daylight attack against the German battleships *Scharnhorst* and *Gneisenau* in harbour at the French Atlantic port of Brest. The attack was reported to be accurate, with the *Gneisenau* seen to be emitting black smoke, but post-raid reconnaissance was inconclusive. A follow-up raid was ordered for the end of the month, although, again, little damage was done. The two raids combined had cost the loss of nine of the fifty-three aircraft involved.

Bennett was now given command of 10 Squadron. The squadron's earlier attacks against the *Gneisenau* and *Scharnhorst* were followed up by attacks against another German battleship, the *Tirpitz,* which was sheltering in a Norwegian fjord near Trondheim – again without success. It had become a hard fought battle between the bomber crews of 4 Group and those of the mighty warships of the Kriegsmarine (the German Navy). During one attack against the *Tirpitz* on the night of 27/28 April 1942, involving thirty-one Halifaxes and a dozen new Lancasters, Bennett's aircraft was hit and the starboard wing set ablaze. With no option other than to bale out, the crew managed to evade capture via neutral Sweden before arriving back at Leeming just over a month later.

At the beginning of May, 77 Squadron moved to Devon on loan to Coastal Command to leave 10 Squadron alone at Leeming once more. Like all Bomber Command squadrons, 10 took part in the Thousand Bomber raids of May and June 1942, flying more than sixty sorties during the three mass raids against Cologne, Essen and Bremen. Then, in August, the squadron finally left Leeming for its new home at Melbourne where it would remain for the rest of the war.

Leeming had been identified to become one of the all-Canadian 6 (RCAF) Group's main airfields, but as the new group had yet to be officially formed it remained an airfield of 4 Group for the time being. However, the first Canadians moved in just days after 10 Squadron had left. The new arrivals were the Wellingtons of 419 (Moose) Squadron, which moved to Yorkshire from Mildenhall where the squadron had been part of 3 Group. The name 'Moose' had been given to 419 when it first formed because of the nickname of its squadron commander, Wing Commander John 'Moose' Fulton, otherwise known as the 'First Mooseman'. Sadly, Fulton had failed to return from a raid on Hamburg but his name lived on. However, within days of 419's arrival at Leeming the squadron moved on, first to Topcliffe and ultimately to Middleton St George where it would spend the rest of the war.

The next Canadians to arrive at Leeming were the advanced party of 408 (Goose) Squadron RCAF, formerly part of 5 Group but now in the process of exchanging its Hampdens for Halifaxes. In October the squadron's conversion flight combined

After a period of substantial redevelopment as a communications hub, RAF Leeming's role today is to support UK and expeditionary air operations, with its Hawks undertaking a multitude of training tasks. (Author)

with another from Topcliffe to form 1659 HCU, tasked with converting new crews to the Halifax, although the HCU had moved out to its new home at Topcliffe by the turn of the year.

In 1943 Leeming was formally transferred to the new 6 (RCAF) Group. The airfield then became Headquarters 63 (RCAF) Base with its sub-stations at Dishforth and Skipton-on-Swale. The HCU's departure had coincided with the arrival of the first members of 405 (Vancouver) Squadron RCAF, although 405 would soon move out to become a Pathfinder unit to make way for 424 (Tiger) Squadron RCAF. But 424 did not stay long at Leeming either. It was on its way to Dalton before its move to the Middle East.

Leeming's next resident squadron, 427 (Lion) Squadron RCAF, arrived from Croft just days later. It was now May 1943 and the squadron was under the command of its first CO, Wing Commander D H Burnside, and was in the process of re-equipping with the Halifax V. The merry-go-round of squadrons that had lasted for almost nine months was just about complete when 429 (Bison) Squadron RCAF replaced 408 Squadron, now on its way to Linton-on-Ouse to convert to the Lancaster II. At last there would be some stability as Leeming would be home to both Canadian Halifax squadrons – 427 and 429 – for the rest of the war.

In September 1943, command of 427 Squadron passed to Wing Commander Robert Turnbull, a former sergeant pilot with a DFM who had recently been awarded the AFC following his tour as an instructor with 1659 HCU. 429 Squadron, meanwhile, was commanded by Wing Commander J D Pattison DFC, a popular character and meticulous when it came to assessing every detail of a raid. Pattison would remain in command of 429 until the end of February 1944 when he was injured during a ground incident involving a canister of incendiaries.

During his time in command Pattison had introduced a number of changes to the way things were normally done on a Halifax bomber squadron. One example was to have the mid-upper turret removed from the squadron's aircraft as a way of reducing weight and so increase the aircraft's performance by, it was estimated, up to 20 mph. It also meant the aircraft could operate slightly higher (by an estimated 1,000 feet). But rather than make the mid-upper gunner redundant, he was used instead in the nose blister of the aircraft to look for any enemy night fighters attacking the bomber from below. The Luftwaffe was now using *Schräge Musik* upward-firing cannons and this had caused fear amongst bomber crews once its existence had become known. This trade-off from losing one of its gun turrets in favour of more speed and an extra lookout was considered by the squadron to be worthwhile.

The tower at Leeming today. (Author)

Pattison was replaced by Wing Commander A F Avant DFC, who took over command of 429 at the beginning of May 1944. The following month command of 427 Squadron passed to Wing Commander G J Cribb as Turnbull returned to Canada with a DFC; he would later return to Yorkshire to command 64 Base and add a Bar to his DFC. Cribb would soon be replaced by E M Bryson who, in turn, was replaced by V F Ganderton, a former member of the squadron, who became the squadron's fourth CO in as many months, although Bryson would later return to resume command of the squadron.

During the final weeks of the war both Leeming squadrons converted to the Lancaster, with the last operation being flown on 25 April 1945 against gun batteries on the island of Wangerooge. With hostilities over, both Canadian squadrons remained in England and were transferred to 1 Group as part of Bomber Command's main force before later disbanding at Leeming at the end of May 1946.

Unlike many of Yorkshire's wartime bomber airfields, Leeming remained very much part of the RAF's post-war plans. After the Lancasters moved out the airfield then became a night fighter base before it was transferred to Training Command in the early 1960s. It continued in this role until the late 1980s when Leeming became a frontline base once again and for twenty years was home to air defence Tornado F3s. During that time Hawks of 100 Squadron moved in but when the last F3 squadron disbanded in 2008 the airfield's future looked uncertain. However, Leeming survived and following a period of substantial redevelopment as a communications hub, RAF Leeming's primary role today is to support UK and expeditionary air operations, with its Hawks undertaking a multitude of training tasks. The station is also home to a force protection wing, a signals unit and a university air squadron, as well as a mountain rescue team. Leeming's past also remains an important part of everyday station life with its excellent Historical Training Facility run by a team of dedicated volunteers.

RAF Leeming is four miles to the south-west of Northallerton and to the south of Leeming Bar on the east side of the A1M. The station is not signposted from the A1M and so when approaching from the south the easiest way to reach the main entrance is by leaving the A1M early (about ten miles south of Leeming Bar at

Preserving the past through its excellent Historical Training Facility is an important part of everyday station life at RAF Leeming. (Author)

the A61 exit) and then by taking the A6055 northwards, which runs parallel to the A1M. You will eventually be able to cross the A1M at the Gatenby roundabout and you will soon see the entrance to RAF Leeming on your left. Equally, if travelling from the north take the A6055 southbound from Leeming Bar.

Summary of units based at Leeming during the Second World War

10 Squadron (ZA) – 8 Jul 40 (Dishforth) – 18 Aug 42 (Melbourne)
Whitley V (Jul 40 – Dec 41)
Halifax II (Dec 41 – Aug 42)

7 Squadron (MG) – 1 Aug 40 (Re-formed) – 28 Oct 40 (Oakington)
Stirling I

102 Squadron (DY) – 25 Aug 40 (Driffield) – 31 Aug 40 (Prestwick)
Whitley V

35 Squadron (TL) – 20 Nov 40 (Boscombe Down) – 4 Dec 40 (Linton-on-Ouse)
Halifax I

77 Squadron (KN) – 5 Sep 41 (Topcliffe) – 5 May 42 (Chivenor)
Whitley V

419 (Moose) Squadron RCAF (VR) – 12 Aug 42 (Mildenhall) – 17 Aug 42 (Topcliffe)
Wellington I/III

408 (Goose) Squadron RCAF (EQ) – 20 Sep 42 (Balderton) – 11 Aug 43 (Linton-on-Ouse)
Hampden I (Sep – Oct 42)
Halifax V (Sep – Dec 42)
Halifax II (Dec 42 – Aug 43)

1659 HCU (FD) – Oct 42 (Formed) – Jan 43 (Topcliffe)
Halifax

405 (Vancouver) Squadron RCAF (LQ) – 14 Mar 43 (Beaulieu) – 17 Apr 43 (Gransden Lodge)
Halifax II

424 (Tiger) Squadron RCAF (QB) – 19 Apr 43 (Topcliffe) – 2 May 43 (Dalton)
Wellington X

427 (Lion) Squadron RCAF (ZL) – 4 May 43 (Croft) – 31 May 46 (Disbanded)
Halifax V (May 43 – Feb 44)
Halifax III (Jan 44 – Mar 45)
Lancaster I/III (Feb 45 – May 46)

429 (Bison) Squadron RCAF (AL) – 12 Aug 43 (East Moor) – 31 May 46 (Disbanded)
Halifax II (Aug 43 – Jan 44)
Halifax V (Oct 43 – Mar 44)
Halifax III (Mar 44 – Mar 45)
Lancaster I/III (Mar 45 – May 46)

CHAPTER 24

Linton-on-Ouse

Location – North Yorkshire, nine miles north-west of York.
Status – Operational airfield. HQ 62 (RCAF) Base.

One of Yorkshire's most famous airfields and still in use by the RAF today is Linton-on-Ouse, arguably Bomber Command's spiritual home in the county. The airfield was home to many different bomber squadrons, first from 4 Group and then from 6 (RCAF) Group, and was unique in that Linton was both a headquarters and an operational airfield for every day of the Second World War. It is also unusual in that during its eighty years of history the airfield has been home to bombers, fighters and training aircraft of the RAF.

Dusk at Linton-on-Ouse during the opening weeks of the war as the Whitleys of 58 Squadron wait for the night's op. (via Ken Delve)

Linton's origins date back to the RAF's Expansion Scheme of the mid-1930s when an area of land on the eastern side of the River Ouse, and adjacent to the north-west corner of the village from which the airfield takes its name, was identified as suitable for development as a large airfield. Because of the area and its size, several minor lanes had to be closed and buildings lost so that the airfield could be built.

Linton-on-Ouse opened in May 1937 as the Headquarters of 4 Group, Bomber Command, under its new AOC, Air Commodore Arthur Harris. Rather unusually for the time, the airfield was constructed with concrete runways and its main facilities, situated on the south-east corner of the airfield adjacent to the village, included five maintenance hangars, as well as many other permanent buildings for domestic and administrative purposes, and enough accommodation for nearly 3,000 personnel.

All this made Linton-on-Ouse one of the RAF's biggest airfields in the north of England and meant that it could be used by two operational squadrons at any one time. Its first station commander was Wing Commander Arthur Pryor, a former

The scars of war – a Whitley of 58 Squadron pictured the morning after a difficult night. (via Ken Delve)

army officer and veteran of the First World War during which he served as a pilot with the Royal Flying Corps. Pryor assumed command of Linton in April 1938, just as the first aircraft arrived. These were two squadrons of Whitleys, 51 and 58 Squadrons, which arrived from Boscombe Down.

Both squadrons were still in residence at the outbreak of the Second World War and on the opening night of hostilities ten aircraft, seven from 58 Squadron and three from 51 Squadron, flew to Leconfield to be loaded with propaganda leaflets, which they then dropped over a dozen German cities, mostly in the industrial heartland of the Ruhr.

Just a month later, 58 Squadron returned to Boscombe Down to work with Coastal Command, leaving 51 Squadron at Linton. The squadron's Whitleys continued to drop leaflets but to avoid such long transits from North Yorkshire detachments of aircraft were sent across the Chanel to operate from airfields in France. 51 Squadron also provided a detachment of aircraft to work with Coastal Command, this time from Kinloss in Scotland, before the squadron left for Dishforth at the end of the year, exchanging places with the Whitley IVs of 78 Squadron.

The new arrivals soon started taking delivery of the Whitley V and in February 1940 were joined by the return of 58 Squadron, also in the process of converting to the Whitley V. Linton's first bombing operations of the war were flown on the night of 18/19 April 1940 when three of 58 Squadron's aircraft joined six other Whitleys to attack enemy shipping off the Oslo and Trondheim areas of Norway, but bad weather prevented most from carrying out their attacks.

As Bomber Command expanded, the headquarters element of 4 Group moved to Heslington Hall to free up space at Linton for its development as a main bomber airfield. During this period, Linton was also home to Lysanders of 4 Squadron, an army co-operation squadron, which had returned to England after the fall of France.

As part of 4 Group's re-organization, 78 Squadron returned to Dishforth, having only just commenced bombing operations, briefly exchanging places with 77 Squadron. But 77 left Linton for its new home at Topcliffe just a month later to be replaced by 102 Squadron. However, 102 Squadron was to be yet another short-term resident as just a month later it was also on its way to

Topcliffe, but one notable pilot to have flown with the squadron during its brief stay at Linton was Leonard Cheshire. Later to be awarded the Victoria Cross, Cheshire was then a young 23-year-old flying officer and was awarded the DSO for getting his badly damaged aircraft back to base after it had been hit during an attack against railway marshalling yards at Cologne on the night of 12/13 November.

Because of the threat of air attacks by the Luftwaffe against Bomber Command's main airfields in Yorkshire, three decoy sites were built for Linton-on-Ouse, at Bossall, Skipsea and Wiggington. By the end of 1940, 58 Squadron had been joined at Linton by 35 Squadron, the first squadron to be equipped with the new four-engine Halifax heavy bomber. The squadron was working up to operational readiness under its first CO, Wing Commander R W P Collings, and by March 1941 was ready to commence operations.

35 Squadron flew its first operational sorties with the Halifax on the night of 10/11 March 1941. The target was the dockyards at Le Havre and just after 7 p.m. six aircraft took off from Linton to join eight Blenheims for the raid. No aircraft were lost during the attack, although one Halifax, L9489 'TL-F' flown by Squadron Leader Peter Gilchrist, was shot down on its way home by an RAF fighter protecting the naval port of Portsmouth during a raid. The intercept took place over Surrey shortly after 10.30 p.m. and sadly it was a case of mistaken identity. Gilchrist and his navigator, Sergeant Ron Aedy, survived but the rest of the crew were killed.

After so many changes since the outbreak of war, things now settled down at Linton-on-Ouse and these two squadrons, 35 and 58, would remain for the next year. They were briefly joined during that time by the Halifaxes of 2 Blind Approach Training Flight, which had formed at Linton in February 1941 but moved out to Driffield just a couple of months later, and 76 Squadron, which re-formed at Linton in May only to move to Middleton St George the following month.

Bomber Command's airfields in eastern England received some unwelcome visitors on the night of 10/11 May 1941 when German intruders crossed the North Sea to pounce on returning RAF bombers and to carry out attacks of opportunity against several bomber airfields. Linton-on-Ouse was one of the airfields to be attacked that night, resulting in significant damage to hangars and buildings, as well as killing thirteen personnel on the ground. Amongst the dead was the station commander, Group Captain Fred Garraway, who was killed near one of the air raid shelters while checking that his personnel were under cover. He is buried in the churchyard at Newton-on-Ouse (All Saints). It was the first of a double tragedy for the Garraway family. His son, 21-year-old Pilot Officer Derek Garraway, would be killed three years later while serving as a bomb aimer with 78 Squadron at Breighton.

One of 35 Squadron's pilots during this period was Leonard Cheshire, now on his second operational tour at Linton-on-Ouse as a flight lieutenant and with a DFC. After completing his tour with 102 Squadron, he had instantly volunteered for a second operational tour and had been posted to the new Halifax with 35 Squadron. His tour ended in early 1942, by which time he had been promoted to the rank of squadron leader, although it would not be his last association with Linton-on-Ouse.

Another legendary pilot to serve with 35 Squadron during this period was Squadron Leader Willie Tait. By the time Tait arrived at Linton to join the squadron he had already been awarded the DSO and he soon added a Bar for leading a daylight raid against the dockyards at Kiel at the end of June 1941; it was the first of his eventual three Bars to his DSO. After completing his tour with 35 Squadron later in the year, he would be rested from operations and posted to a training unit; but it would not be for long.

The Halifaxes of 35 Squadron took part in attacks against three of the German mighty warships, *Scharnhorst*, *Gneisenau* and *Prinz Eugen*, during the infamous Channel dash of February 1942. Using surprise and bad weather as a tactic, the ships sailed from the French Atlantic port of Brest under the protection of a huge armada of ships and an umbrella of fighter cover from the Luftwaffe. Together with their escorts, the *Scharnhorst*, *Gneisenau* and *Prinz Eugen* all passed safely through the English Channel in broad daylight, right under the noses of the British, to make their way home to ports in northern Germany.

Then, in March and April, the squadron was involved in two unsuccessful attacks against the mighty German battleship *Tirpitz*, lying in a Norwegian fjord. The first attempt, carried out by thirty-four Halifaxes on 30/31 March, failed to locate the *Tirpitz*. The second, carried out on 27/28 April, involved thirty-one Halifaxes and twelve Lancasters. The bombers had first flown to northern Scotland from where the raid was carried out, but although the *Tirpitz* was found and bombed, no hits were achieved. Four Halifaxes and one Lancaster failed to return.

One of the Halifaxes lost that night was W1048 'TL-S' of 35 Squadron flown by Pilot Officer Donald McIntyre. He had taken off from Kinloss at 8.30 p.m. but having found the *Tirpitz* more than four hours later the Halifax was hit by anti-aircraft fire. With the aircraft on fire and the crew unable to extinguish it, McIntyre was faced with no option other than to try and bring the aircraft down. But in mountainous terrain there was nowhere to crash-land and so he attempted to sit the blazing bomber down on a frozen lake. With immense skill, McIntyre touched the aircraft down with its undercarriage still retracted. The aircraft skidded across the ice, still on fire, before finally coming to rest. It would soon sink through the ice. Remarkably, though, all on board survived and six of the crew eventually evaded through neutral Sweden, while one, the flight engineer, Sergeant Vic Stevens, who had been injured in the crash, was later captured to become a prisoner of war. The Halifax had come down on Lake Hoklingen in Norway and thirty-one years later was raised and taken to the shore by an RAF sub-aqua expedition and members of a local diving club. The aircraft was then returned to the UK and put on public display at the RAF Museum Hendon.

During this period, 35 Squadron was under the command of Jimmy Marks, who had taken over from Wing Commander B V Robinson in March 1942. The tall and fair-haired Marks was a popular and young CO from Sawbridgeworth. He was also a courageous leader and had already been awarded the DSO and DFC having flown more than fifty operational sorties by the age of twenty-three. Marks would later add a Bar to his DSO but would sadly lose his life later in the year while leading the squadron during a raid on Saarbrucken. At the time of his death Jimmy Marks was aged twenty-four.

By now the Whitley's operational days were coming to an end and so 58 Squadron moved to Cornwall on its transfer to Coastal Command. The Halifaxes of 35 Squadron, meanwhile, pressed on from Linton-on-Ouse, taking part in the three Thousand Bomber raids against Cologne, Essen and Bremen during May and June, before being selected to be 4 Group's contribution to the new Pathfinders in August 1942.

The departure of 35 Squadron signalled the return of 76 and 78 Squadrons to Linton-on-Ouse, both equipped with the Halifax II. Also returning to Linton was Leonard Cheshire, who had just taken command of 76 Squadron. Remarkably, he had only just celebrated his twenty-fifth birthday but he was now starting his third operational tour as a bomber pilot.

Cheshire proved to be a meticulous but popular commanding officer, getting to know everyone under his command and spending time with his crews working out how to get the best out of them and their aircraft. Cheshire remained in command of 76 Squadron until April 1943 when he left on promotion to become station commander at Marston Moor as the RAF's youngest group captain and with a Bar to his DSO.

Cheshire's departure from Linton coincided with the height of the Battle of the Ruhr, a particularly hard and costly campaign for the station's two Halifax squadrons. The campaign against Germany's industrial heartland lasted four months and resulted in more than fifty aircraft failing to return to Linton. One of those lost was an aircraft of 76 Squadron flown by 26-year-old Flight Lieutenant Arthur Hull. His aircraft was shot down by an enemy night fighter during a raid against Frankfurt on the night of 10/11 April. Hull was killed but flying with him as second pilot that night was Linton's station commander, Group Captain John Whitley, who managed to bale out and evade capture. He eventually returned to England via Gibraltar to become station commander at Lissett, after which he commanded 43 Base before becoming 4 Group's AOC for the final few months of the war.

Meanwhile, Linton-on-Ouse had been earmarked as a base for the new Canadian 6 (RCAF) Group and so both 76 and 78 Squadrons moved out during June 1943. The first Canadian unit to arrive was 426 (Thunderbird) Squadron RCAF under the command of 33-year-old Wing Commander Leslie Crooks DSO DFC, which arrived from Dishforth.

The following month Linton was officially transferred to 6 (RCAF) Group and designated Headquarters 62 (RCAF) Base with its sub-stations at East Moor and Tholthorpe. The

Thunderbirds immediately began replacing their Wellingtons with Lancaster IIs and took part in 6 (RCAF) Group's first Lancaster operations of the war on the night of 17/18 August, when nine of its aircraft were part of a main force of nearly 600 aircraft carrying out an attack against the German V-weapons research establishment at Peenemünde on the Baltic coast.

Although the raid is believed to have set the Nazi's V-weapons programme back by an estimated two months, success had come at a cost for Bomber Command. Forty aircraft were lost that night, mostly from the third wave after the Luftwaffe's night fighters arrived. The worst of the losses, in percentage terms, were suffered by the Canadians of 6 (RCAF) Group. Of the group's fifty-seven aircraft taking part, twelve did not return; more than 20 per cent. Two of those shot down were from 426 Squadron. One was 'OW-M' flown by Flight Lieutenant Doug Shuttleworth, an experienced pilot from Saskatchewan with a DFC and twenty ops already behind him. Most of Shuttleworth's crew were of similar experience but they had picked up a new flight engineer when the crew had converted to the Lancaster, Sergeant Syd Barnes, who was on his first op. Nothing was heard from the crew again. The second loss was 'OW-V' flown by the squadron commander, Leslie Crooks. His body and four of his crew were found in the wreckage. Only one of his crew, Sergeant K W Reading, survived to become a prisoner of war. It appears that the navigator, 21-year-old Flight Sergeant Alfred Howes, had managed to get out of the aircraft only to fall to his death when his parachute failed to open; he was on his third op. The flight engineer, Sergeant John Hislop, a young Scot was also aged twenty-one and flying his first op. Also experiencing an operation for the first time was the mid-upper gunner, 20-year-old Pilot Officer Theo Dos Santos from Trinidad. Leslie Crooks was the squadron's second CO to be killed in action and he is buried with his crew in the Berlin 1939–1945 War Cemetery.

With the loss of Crooks, command of the Thunderbirds passed to Wing Commander Bill Swetman. It was now the start of the long and costly campaign against Berlin and the Halifaxes of 426 Squadron were involved from the outset. The squadron was now joined at Linton by 408 (Goose) Squadron RCAF, which moved in from Leeming and immediately exchanged its Halifaxes for Lancasters.

Linton had been selected as 6 (RCAF) Group's main Lancaster base and the two squadrons flew operationally together for the first time on the night of 7/8 October 1943. The target was Stuttgart and it was an all-Lancaster effort by Bomber Command involving nearly 350 aircraft from across five groups (1, 3, 5, 6 and 8 Groups). Twenty-eight aircraft were from Linton-on-Ouse, fourteen from each squadron. Diversionary attacks by supporting Mosquitos had confused the German defences to the point that only a few enemy night fighters were encountered around the target area. Although cloud over Stuttgart meant that bombing was only moderately successful, just four Lancasters failed to return; this was 1 per cent of the attacking force, a remarkably low loss rate for that stage of the war.

Being Lancaster-equipped, both of Linton's resident squadrons were heavily involved in the long and costly campaign against Berlin during the hard winter of 1943/44. Of the sixteen major raids flown against the Nazi capital, the two Linton-based squadrons were involved in all but one.

The station was now under the command of Air Commodore Dwight Ross, the former station commander of Middleton St George, who took command of 62 (RCAF) Base on promotion in February 1944. The Lancaster II was now being phased out of service to be replaced by the Halifax III, with 426 Squadron being the first of Linton's squadrons to convert, having flown its last Lancaster operations during early May. For a while 408 remained one of just two Bomber Command squadrons operating the Lancaster II. One notable loss during this period was the squadron commander, 29-year-old Wing Commander David Jacobs DFC from Toronto, who was killed during a raid against Dortmund on the night of 22/23 May. He was the squadron's second CO to have been killed whilst at Linton after his predecessor, 28-year-old Wing Commander Alex Mair DFC from Ontario, had been killed the previous November during the early exchanges of the Battle of Berlin.

408 Squadron was still operating the Lancaster when both Linton squadrons supported the Allied landings in Normandy. Finally, in September 1944, the squadron began replacing its Lancs with Halifaxes, initially Mark IIIs and then Mark VIIs, and it was the Halifax VII that would still be serving with both Linton squadrons at the end of the war.

Sadly, there were still losses to come before hostilities in Europe were over and one bad night for Linton was just weeks before the end of the war, on the night of 5/6 March 1945, when 426 Squadron lost three of its fourteen Halifaxes soon after taking off for a raid against Chemnitz. One collided with another Halifax that had just taken off from Tholthorpe, while the other two seemingly stalled after suffering severe icing and came down in the local vicinity.

As with other Halifax squadrons, the last operations of the war from Linton were flown on 25 April 1945 against gun batteries on the Frisian island of Wangerooge. Although it was the group's last operation of the war, it was not without tragedy. Five of the 300-plus Halifaxes taking part in the raid failed to return, four of which were involved in collisions over the target. These included two aircraft from Linton-on-Ouse, one each from 408 and 426 Squadrons, with the loss of all fourteen men on board.

Although hostilities were over in Europe, the war in the Far East raged on. 408 Squadron was allocated to Tiger Force and so converted to the Canadian-built Lancaster X but within weeks the war with Japan was over and the squadron disbanded. 426 Squadron, however, was to survive the post-war axe and like a number of Halifax squadrons was transferred to Transport

Retained in the post-war RAF, Linton-on-Ouse has been home to many types over the years – transport aircraft, fighters and helicopters – but for many years it has been home to the Tucano. Linton remains one of the RAF's busiest airfields, tasked with the training of future fast jet pilots. (Author)

The wartime air traffic control tower has survived and is still used today, although it has taken on a slightly different appearance. (Author)

Command and moved to Driffield. The Thunderbirds were briefly replaced by 405 (Vancouver) Squadron RCAF, also allocated to Tiger Force and equipped with the Lancaster X, but, like 408, the new arrivals soon disbanded once the war in the Far East had come to an end.

Linton-on-Ouse was retained in the post-war RAF and was home to many types – transport aircraft, fighters and helicopters – until the late-1950s when the airfield was transferred to Flying Training Command and became home to No. 1 Flying Training School, the oldest military flying training school in the world. Today, RAF Linton-on-Ouse is home to the Tucano T1 and remains one of the RAF's busiest airfields, tasked with the training of future fast jet pilots for the Royal Air Force and Royal Navy.

RAF Linton-on-Ouse is nine miles north-west of York, to the west of the A19. When travelling northbound, leave the A19 at Shipton by Beningbrough. Alternatively, if approaching from the west, via the A1/A59, the RAF station is signposted by heading towards Great Ouseburn and then by crossing the River Ouse towards the airfield. Several reminders can be found on station of the airfield's wartime past, including the original control tower. Furthermore, a well maintained and most informative Memorial Room is located in the former airmen's mess. It was created to honour all those who have served at Linton-on-Ouse

In front of the station headquarters at Linton-on-Ouse is a memorial to the station's personnel killed while serving on the ground, including the thirteen who lost their lives during the air raid on the night of 11/12 May 1941. (Author)

and its satellites in peace and war, and contains a wide variety of photographs and artefacts from the wartime era as well as displays covering Linton's post-war history. From figures compiled by its curator, Linton's squadrons flew on more than a thousand raids during the Second World War (nearly 10,000 individual sorties),

Most of today's RAF stations have preserved their past and Linton-on-Ouse is no exception. Its wonderful Memorial Room, run by volunteers, is located in the former airmen's mess. (Author)

A memorial cairn can be found in the village of Linton-on-Ouse. It was erected by the associations and former members of 408 and 426 Squadrons and the people of the village, and dedicated to the Canadians who served at the airfield in the final two years of the war. (Author)

during which more than 350 aircraft were lost with the loss of 1,235 lives. A memorial to the station's personnel killed while serving on the ground, including the thirteen who lost their lives during the enemy attack on Linton-on-Ouse on the night of 11/12 May 1941, can be found outside the station headquarters. Access to RAF Linton-on-Ouse is by prior permission only.

In addition to the reminders of this airfield's wartime past on station, a memorial cairn can be found in the village of Linton-on-Ouse. It was erected by the associations and former members of 408 and 426 Squadrons and the people of the village, and dedicated in 1990 to the Canadians who served at the airfield in the final two years of the war. On leaving the RAF station turn left at the T-junction in the village. The cairn is just a hundred yards or so on your right outside the village hall.

Summary of units based at Linton-on-Ouse during the Second World War

51 Squadron (MB) – 20 Apr 38 (Boscombe Down) – 8 Dec 39 (Dishforth)
Whitley II

58 Squadron (GE) – 20 Apr 38 (Boscombe Down) – 5 Oct 39 (Boscombe Down)
Whitley II/II

78 Squadron (EY) – 15 Oct 39 (Dishforth) – 14 Jul 40 (Dishforth)
Whitley II/V

58 Squadron (GE) – 14 Feb 40 (Boscombe Down) – 7 Apr 42 (St Eval)
Whitley V

77 Squadron (KN) – 28 Aug 40 (Driffield) – 4 Oct 40 (Topcliffe)
Whitley V

102 Squadron (DY) – 10 Oct 40 (Prestwick) – 14 Nov 40 (Topcliffe)
Whitley V

35 Squadron (TL) – 5 Dec 40 (Leeming) – 14 Aug 42 (Graveley)
Halifax I (Dec 40 – Feb 42)
Halifax II (Feb – Aug 42)

76 Squadron (MP) – 1 May 41 (Re-formed) – 3 Jun 41 (Middleton St George)
Halifax I

78 Squadron (EY) – 16 Sep 42 (Middleton St George) – 15 Jun 43 (Breighton)
Halifax II

76 Squadron (MP) – 17 Sep 42 (Re-formed) – 15 Jun 43 (Holme-on-Spalding Moor)
Halifax II (Sep 42 – Apr 43)
Halifax V (Apr – Jun 43)

426 (Thunderbird) Squadron RCAF (OW) – 18 Jun 43 (Dishforth) – 24 May 45 (Driffield)
Wellington X (May – Jun 43)
Lancaster II (Jun 43 – May 44)
Halifax III (Apr – Jun 44)
Halifax VII (Jun 44 – May 45)

408 (Goose) Squadron RCAF (EQ) – 12 Aug 43 (Leeming) – 14 Jun 45 (Disbanded)
Halifax II (Aug – Sep 43)
Lancaster II (Oct 43 – Jul 44)
Halifax III (Jul 44 – Feb 45)
Halifax VII (Feb – May 45)
Lancaster X (May – Jun 45)

405 (Vancouver) Squadron RCAF (LQ) – 26 May 45 (Gransden Lodge) – 16 Jun 45 (Disbanded)
Lancaster X

CHAPTER 25

Middleton St George (Goosepool)

Location – County Durham, five miles east of Darlington.
Status – Operational airfield. HQ 64 (RCAF) Base.

Now the site of Durham Tees Valley Airport, the history of this airfield once known as Middleton St George, the most northerly of Bomber Command's airfields, dates back to before the Second World War when land was identified

Andrew Mynarski, a mid-upper gunner serving with 419 (Moose) Squadron at Middleton St George, was posthumously awarded the Victoria Cross for his extreme courage on the night of 12/13 June 1944. Having been attacked by an enemy night fighter, a fire raged on board his Lancaster but instead of saving himself the gallant Mynarski went to the aid of his colleague trapped inside the rear turret. The rear gunner survived but Mynarski later died from his horrific injuries. (AHB)

for development to the east of the village by which the airfield would eventually take its name. To locals, though, the airfield was often referred to as Goosepool, after a nearby farm, but this name was never officially used.

Although land had first been identified during the RAF's expansion of the mid-1930s, progress was slow. Construction of the airfield was clearly not a priority and so work did not begin until just before the outbreak of war. Middleton St George finally opened in January 1941 and was allocated to 4 Group. It had been completed to the standard bomber design, with three hardened runways; the main runway being 2,000 yards long and running from the north-east corner of the airfield to the south-west. The thirty-six aircraft dispersals were mainly situated on the eastern and south-eastern parts of the airfield, but facilities were limited for its 2,500 personnel, particularly when it came to aircraft maintenance. Only two hangars were initially erected on the technical site, situated in the north-west corner of the airfield, although three more would later be constructed before the end of the war.

The first aircraft to arrive were Whitleys of 78 Squadron, which arrived from Dishforth in April 1941 under the command of 29-year-old Wing Commander Basil Robinson. Born in Tyne and Wear, Robinson was no stranger to the north-east. He was a keen rugby player and had joined the RAF in 1933, and had now worked his way up to command a squadron on home soil. Within days of its arrival, the squadron was in action and soon after was joined by 76 Squadron, equipped with the new Halifax four-engine heavy bomber, which arrived from Linton-on-Ouse during the early days of June. The new arrivals were also soon in action and suffered their first loss from Middleton on the night of 23/24 June during a raid against the port of Kiel. Twenty-six aircraft had taken part in the raid, and the Halifax, flown by Pilot Officer Walter Stobbs, was the only loss. The crew are buried in Becklingen War Cemetery in northern Germany.

For a while the two squadrons operated from Middleton together, 78 with the Whitley and 76 the Halifax, until a satellite airfield at Croft was ready to receive its first squadron. The unit leaving was Basil Robinson's 78 Squadron, which flew its last operation with the Whitley in October and then left for Croft to prepare to receive its first Halifax.

As things turned out, 78 Squadron was not away for long as it returned to Middleton in June 1942 with its Halifax IIs to replace 76 Squadron, now destined for the Middle East. Command of 78 Squadron had recently passed to Wing Commander Willie Tait DSO DFC, a man who would later become a legend within Bomber Command having been decorated six times, including three Bars to his DSO. But 78 Squadron's second stint at Middleton was not to last long, just three months in fact, as by September it had followed 76 out of the door.

Middleton St George was to become a main airfield for the new Canadian 6 (RCAF) Group about to form. The first Canadians to arrive were Wellingtons of 420 (Snowy Owl) Squadron RCAF, which arrived from Skipton-on-Swale in October, followed by the much-travelled 419 (Moose) Squadron from Croft the following month. This latter squadron had been formed just a year before and was now in the process of converting to the Halifax II but it had been moved from pillar to post since its formation and Middleton was to be its fifth home. But at last the crews could settle as Middleton St George would be 419's home for the rest of the war. The airfield was also briefly home to Airspeed Oxfords, initially of 1516 BAT Flight and then the newly formed 1535 BATF, which replaced 1516, but as the Canadian squadrons built-up, and with space tight at the airfield, both units moved out in early 1943.

Middleton St George was now formally part of 6 (RCAF) Group, with the two Canadian squadrons fully immersed in operations, and when the RAF re-structured its organization of airfields, Middleton became Headquarters 64 (RCAF) Base, with its sub-station at Croft, under the overall command of Group Captain Dwight Ross. Aged thirty-five and a pre-war officer with the RCAF, Ross had only recently arrived in England having spent the previous two years in command of a flying training school in Canada under the British Commonwealth Air Training Plan, a programme for the training of British and Commonwealth aircrew during the Second World War.

In May 1943, the Snowy Owls moved to North Africa to be replaced by 428 (Ghost) Squadron RCAF, previously a 4 Group squadron but now transferred to 6 (RCAF) Group. The new arrivals had moved in from Dalton during early June and like 419 Squadron, would remain at Middleton for the rest of the war.

428 Squadron was then under the command of Wing Commander D W N Smith, but Smith would not complete his tour of operations and would instead see out hostilities as a prisoner of war after he and his crew escaped with their lives on the night of 15/16 September. Flying a Halifax V, LK913 'NA-N Nan', and with a second pilot on board, Smith and his crew had taken off from Middleton just before 8 pm to join a raiding force of 369 aircraft. They were on their way to the Dunlop rubber factory at Montluçon. The Pathfinders had done a good job in illuminating the target and after dropping his bombs, Smith turned for home. But it was then that his aircraft was hit by incendiaries dropped from an aircraft above. As Smith struggled to regain some control, two of his crew baled out but the others remained on board and Smith eventually managed to force-land his aircraft in a plantation near Sérilly, to the south-east of Paris. Four of the crew managed to evade and with the help of the French Resistance they eventually made their way back to England, but Smith and three others were captured.

With Smith now a prisoner of war, command of the squadron was temporarily passed to Squadron Leader William Suggitt before Wing Commander D T French arrived at the end of October. Following the hard-fought Battle of Berlin during the winter of 1943/44, both Middleton squadrons converted to the Canadian-built Lancaster X, which they would retain until the end of the war. Both squadrons were then involved in the build-up to the Allied landings of D-Day and the subsequent breakout into northern France.

These latter missions involved attacks against enemy lines of communications, such as vital rail links and marshalling yards, and on the night of 12/13 June 1944, Middleton's Lancasters were part of a large force of more than 670 aircraft sent to attack such targets in northern France. One of 419's sixteen aircraft taking part in the raid that night was flown by Flying Officer Arthur de Breyne. It was his tenth op, two more than the rest of his crew having earlier flown two additional sorties as a second pilot at the start of his tour.

The crew's target that night was the railway marshalling yards at Cambrai. Being summer and with it being a relatively short distance to the target, take-off from Middleton was late. It was nearly 10 p.m. before the crew got airborne and as they crossed the French coast they found the weather to be good, with little or no protection from any marauding night fighters. As they began their run-in towards the target they were greeted by heavy flak but de Breyne held the aircraft steady. Closer and closer they got but then, without warning, a Ju 88 night fighter was spotted on their port side, guns blazing against the dark night sky and raking the Lancaster from below and slightly astern.

The attack had been devastating. Both of the Lancaster's port engines had been taken out and a fire was soon raging inside the rear of the fuselage, fuelled by leaking hydraulic fluid and trapping the rear gunner, George Brophy, in his turret. The Lancaster's turrets were powered by hydraulics provided by the aircraft's engines and in the case of the rear turret, power came from the port outer engine. In this case, with the engine out, hydraulic power was not available but the turret had still been designed to be operated manually by the rear gunner – but as Brophy frantically turned the handle, it broke. The turret had jammed in a position that left Brophy trapped. He could not get out, no matter how hard he tried, and he was now faced with a slow and painful death. Meanwhile, de Breyne had given the order to his crew to bale out. He had no choice.

In the mid-upper turret, 27-year-old Warrant Officer Andrew Mynarski climbed down from his position to make his way towards the forward escape hatch. As he did so he noticed Brophy still trapped in the rear turret. Mynarski could so easily have saved himself but instead he went aft to fight the fire. Using a fire axe, Andy Mynarski did all that he could to pry the turret doors apart or to get the turret to move to give Brophy the chance to make his escape, but it was no good. The turret was well and truly jammed. Furthermore, Mynarski's flying clothing and parachute were now on fire but he still did not give up, doing all that he could to beat the flames with his hands. Brophy knew that his fate was sealed and could see that Mynarski would go the same way and so he waved his colleague away. Reluctantly, Mynarski turned away but before making his own escape he was last seen saluting the trapped gunner as a gesture of farewell. Mynarski jumped but his clothing and parachute were still on fire and he fell to earth in flames. He was later found by local French farmers and was still alive at that time, but his body was so badly burned that he soon died from his horrific injuries.

The Lancaster came down on farmland and broke up on impact. The rear turret, still with Brophy inside, broke free and, remarkably, he survived; as did the other members of the crew. Brophy was found by the French and he later returned to England, as did the other survivors of the crew, and it was then that the full story of what had happened on board the Lancaster became known. Soon after came the announcement that Andrew Mynarski was to be posthumously awarded the Victoria Cross. It was the first of three VCs to Canadian airmen during the Second World War, although it was the last of the three to be promulgated in the London Gazette.

One of 419 Squadron's aircraft during this period was KB700 'VR-Z', known as the *Ruhr Express*, which had been the first Canadian-built Lancaster X, but unfortunately it came to grief on the night of 2/3 January 1945 when it crash-landed back at Middleton after returning from a raid against Nuremberg. It was the aircraft's forty-ninth op.

The last missions of the war from Middleton St George were flown on 25 April 1945 when each squadron provided fifteen aircraft for the attack against gun batteries on the Frisian island

The St George Hotel at Durham Tees Valley Airport was formerly the officers' mess for Middleton St George. Outside the front of the hotel is a memorial stone to honour the three Canadian squadrons that flew from the airfield during the Second World War and a marvellous statue of Pilot Officer Andrew Mynarski VC. (Author)

On entering the airport's complex at Durham Tees Valley there are several original buildings to be found. This one, for example, is now used as the International Fire Training Centre. (Author)

of Wangerooge. Then, with an end to hostilities in Europe, both squadrons were allocated to Tiger Force and returned to Canada in preparation for a move to the Far East, but after the Japanese surrender both squadrons were disbanded in early September.

With both of its Canadian bomber squadrons gone, Middleton St George briefly transferred to Fighter Command and then Flying Training Command before reverting again to Fighter Command during the mid-1950s. It remained a fighter airfield until 1964 when the RAF's rationalization of its airfields meant that Middleton St George was surplus to requirement. Given the amount of post-war financial investment, the decision to close the airfield to military flying came as something of a surprise but this former wartime airfield still had a bright future when the land was purchased by the former Cleveland County Council, which saw the airfield's potential as a commercial airport. Today, although still often referred to by its previous name of Teesside International Airport, Durham Tees Valley Airport is one of Britain's smaller domestic airports but also offers links to a number of European destinations.

The airport is between Darlington and Middlesbrough, to the south of the A66 and on the eastern side of the village of Middleton St George. Entry to the airport is from the A67, which runs to the south and parallel to the main A66. As you enter the airport's complex there are several former wartime buildings to be found. If you bear left at the first mini-roundabout, the road takes you through what was the airfield's administrative site. These buildings are still being used today, for example one is used as the International Fire Training Centre. By continuing along the road and bearing right, the road takes you to the St George Hotel, formerly the officers' mess. Outside the front of the hotel is a memorial stone to honour the three Canadian squadrons that flew from Middleton St George during the Second World War between 1942 and 1945, and a marvellous statue of Pilot Officer Andrew Mynarski VC.

Summary of units based at Middleton St George during the Second World War

78 Squadron (EY) – 7 Apr 41 (Dishforth) – 19 Oct 41 (Croft)
Whitley V

76 Squadron (MP) – 4 Jun 41 (Linton-on-Ouse) – 12 Jul 42 (Middle East)
Halifax I (Jun 41 – Feb 42)
Halifax II (Oct 41 – Jul 42)

78 Squadron (EY) – 10 Jun 42 (Croft) – 15 Sep 42 (Linton-on-Ouse)
Halifax II

420 (Snowy Owl) Squadron RCAF (PT) – 15 Oct 42 (Skipton-on-Swale) – 16 May 43 (North Africa)
Wellington III (Oct 42 – Apr 43)
Wellington X (Feb – May 43)

419 (Moose) Squadron RCAF (VR) – 9 Nov 42 (Croft) – 4 Jun 45 (Disbanded)
Halifax II (Nov 42 – Mar 44)
Lancaster X (Mar 44 – Jun 45)

428 (Ghost) Squadron RCAF (NA) – 4 Jun 43 (Dalton) – 31 May 45 (Disbanded)
Halifax V (Jun 43 – Jan 44)
Halifax III (Nov 43 – Jun 44)
Lancaster X (Jun 44 – May 45)

Chapter 26

Skipton-on-Swale

Location – North Yorkshire, four miles west of Thirsk.
Status – Satellite airfield. 63 (RCAF) Base – sub-station of Leeming.

Another of Yorkshire's Canadian wartime airfields, and home to four RCAF squadrons at various stages of the war, was Skipton-on-Swale. The need for more bomber airfields in eastern England led to work beginning in 1941 to construct a satellite airfield for Leeming. The new airfield was built on land that was effectively squeezed by the River Swale, the village of Skipton-on-Swale and the Northallerton Road. Nonetheless, it was completed to the standard three-runway bomber airfield design, with the main runway being 1,900 yards long and running from the north-east to the south-west of the airfield, and with the construction of three hangars for aircraft maintenance and enough accommodation for 2,000 personnel.

By the autumn of 1942, although still far from complete, enough work had been completed to allow Skipton-on-Swale to receive its first squadron. Skipton was always destined for the Canadians, but the all-Canadian 6 (RCAF) Group had yet to form and so the airfield was initially allocated to 4 Group. The first squadron to arrive was 420 (Snowy Owl) Squadron RCAF, which was in the process of exchanging its Hampdens for the newer and more capable Wellington III.

Life at Skipton was to be very different for the new arrivals. They had come from Waddington in Lincolnshire, one of the RAF's permanent airfields where facilities had been good for its personnel, particularly the domestic and administrative facilities on base, but now they were to experience life on a

432 (Leaside) Squadron RCAF formed at Skipton-on-Swale in May 1943 but its Wellingtons soon moved out to make way for Halifaxes belonging to two more Canadian squadrons. (AHB)

temporary wartime airfield where the facilities were basic and spread over a large area.

The squadron flew its first op with the Wellington on the night of 5/6 October 1942. The target was Aachen and more than 250 aircraft took part, a mixed force of Wellingtons, Lancasters, Halifaxes and Stirlings. The crews found the weather over much of north-west Europe to be particularly bad. There was little the newly formed Pathfinders could do to help mark the target and so bombing was scattered. All of Skipton's aircraft returned safely, although ten aircraft from other squadrons had failed to return and a further six crash-landed back in eastern England due to the bad weather.

Many of those serving with 420 Squadron at the time would have been glad to learn that their stay at Skipton was not to last long. With Bomber Command shuffling its pack, the Snowy Owls were on their way to Middleton St George and so for more than six months Skipton-on-Swale was left without a resident squadron. With more construction work going on the airfield was not officially transferred to the newly formed 6 (RCAF) Group until the spring of 1943.

It took a while for the Canadian group to build up in size and so it was not until the beginning of May 1943 that the airfield had a resident squadron once more. This was 432 (Leaside) Squadron RCAF, which formed at Skipton with most of its crews coming from Croft where they had been serving with 427 (Lion) Squadron.

Under the command of 26-year-old Wing Commander Harry Kerby, 432 Squadron was the twelfth Canadian squadron to have been formed overseas but the first to have been formed under 6 (RCAF) Group. Equipped with Canadian-built Wellington Xs and consisting of many experienced crews, it was not long before the new squadron was ready to commence operations.

The squadron flew its first op on the night of 23/24 May 1943 when fifteen aircraft joined a raid against Dortmund. It was the first major raid by Bomber Command following a nine-day break after 617 Squadron had flown the legendary Dams Raid. With the Main Force squadrons having had a break, it was a large attacking force of 826 aircraft – a mix of Lancasters, Halifaxes, Wellingtons, Stirlings and Mosquitos – and it proved to be a successful night. Weather conditions in the target area were favourable, meaning the Pathfinders were able to accurately mark the target, and resulted in devastation across large parts of the city. All of Skipton's aircraft returned safely.

It had been a good start to operational life at Skipton for the new squadron but its early luck would soon run out. The Battle of the Ruhr was hard fought on both sides and Bomber Command's raids against the industrial heartland of Nazi Germany were big. So, too, were its losses. Just four nights later the target was Essen with more than 500 bombers involved. The weather was cloudy, again resulting in scattered bombing, and amongst the twenty-three aircraft lost that night was a Wellington from Skipton flown by Pilot Officer Ralph Taylor, a 26-year-old from Northern Ireland who had been awarded the DFM during his previous tour. What happened to Taylor and his crew is not known but they became the squadron's first operational casualties and are remembered on the Runnymede Memorial.

Sadly, Harry Kerby would also be killed soon after. He failed to return from a raid against Hamburg on the night of 29/30 July. Kerby was replaced by Wing Commander W A McKay. Unlike many of Yorkshire's bomber squadrons, 432 was not to receive the Halifax but was instead to convert to the Lancaster and so in September it moved to East Moor in preparation for receiving its new aircraft. This time, Skipton was not to remain dormant for long. Within days 433 (Porcupine) Squadron RCAF had formed under the command of Wing Commander Clive Sinton.

With the arrival of the first four-engine Halifaxes, Skipton-on-Swale now moved to a new era of operating heavy bombers, although the first heavy bomber operations would not be flown from the airfield until the night of 2/3 January 1944 when three of the squadron's Halifaxes dropped mines off the Frisian Islands. The squadron's first bombing op was flown soon after when eight of its aircraft went to Berlin for the first time; fortunately, all aircraft returned safely. However, the next visit to the Big City, on the night of 28/29 January, resulted in the loss of three squadron aircraft.

By now, the Porcupines had been joined at Skipton by the Tigers of 424 Squadron RCAF. The Tigers had returned from overseas in early November to equip with the Halifax and to join Bomber Command's Main Force. Under the command of Wing Commander Arthur Martin, 424 Squadron had flown its first op from Skipton on the night of 20/21 January but it had been a real baptism of fire for the Tigers. Amongst Bomber Command's losses that night was the crew of Arthur Martin. His aircraft was one of twenty-two Halifaxes lost that night.

Sadly, the end of the Battle of Berlin did not bring an end to the suffering; far from it. Three more aircraft were lost from Skipton during the disastrous Nuremberg raid at the end of March 1944. Two were lost from 424 Squadron while the third, HX272, belonged to 433. It was shot down by a night fighter near the target. Although three of the crew survived, one of the five to have been killed was the crew's flight engineer, Pilot Officer Christopher Panton from Lincolnshire. The significance of Panton's death became apparent many years later when in 1988 his two brothers, Fred and Harold Panton, opened the Lincolnshire Aviation Heritage Centre at the former Bomber Command airfield of East Kirkby in Lincolnshire as a living tribute to their older brother and the 55,000 men who died whilst serving with Bomber Command during the Second World War.

Under the re-organization of RAF airfields, Skipton-on-Swale had become a sub-station of 63 (RCAF) Base, headquartered at Leeming. Both Canadian squadrons, 433 and 424, would operate side-by-side from Skipton-on-Swale for the rest of the war and both were involved in supporting the Allied landings in Normandy on D-Day, 6 June 1944, and the subsequent breakout from the beachhead.

Following the death of Arthur Martin, 424 Squadron had been taken over by Wing Commander John Blane from Ontario, but he, too, was killed while leading the squadron; his death came on his twelfth operational sortie, against Hamburg at the end of July 1944. Command of the squadron now passed to Wing Commander G A Roy, but he would not see out his tour at Skipton. Roy was shot down during a raid against Bochum on the night of 9/10 October to become a prisoner of war. Roy was replaced by Wing Commander C C W Marshall who would lead 424 until just before the end of the war, by which time both Skipton squadrons had exchanged their Halifaxes for Lancasters, their conversion having begun in January 1945.

The last Halifax lost from Skipton occurred on the night of 28/29 January 1945. The aircraft, LW164 'QB-C', belonged to 424 Squadron and was on its sixty-eighth op. It was flown that night by Wing Commander Ed Williams AFC. At 7.20 p.m. Williams began the take-off run bound for Stuttgart but as the aircraft was getting airborne it swung out of control and crashed in a ball of flames. Remarkably, the tail gunner, Flying Officer J E H B Tremblay, escaped with his life and although critically injured he was rushed to Northallerton hospital. The other six crew members on board were all killed. Williams and his colleagues are buried in the Harrogate (Stonefall) Cemetery.

The last ops from Skipton were flown on the Wangerooge raid on 25 April 1945 with each squadron providing ten aircraft; all returned safely. During Skipton's operational existence, ninety-eight aircraft had failed to return; two-thirds of which were Halifaxes. With the war over, both squadrons remained at Skipton and were transferred to 1 Group to take part in ferrying British troops back home from the Mediterranean theatre, before the squadrons were disbanded in October 1945. With no further requirement for Skipton-on-Swale in the post-war RAF, the airfield then closed and over the years since the land has reverted to agriculture and farming.

This former wartime airfield is four miles west of Thirsk and immediately to the north of the village of Skipton-on-Swale; the village marking the airfield's southernmost point.

A memorial stone on the village green at Skipton-on-Swale is dedicated to the four Canadian squadrons that flew from the airfield during the Second World War. The cairn is in the shade of a Canadian maple tree and marks the point where a crippled Halifax of 433 Squadron came down in August 1944 having returned from a bombing mission, killing two of the crew as well as a young boy who was caught in the wreckage. (Author)

The River Swale runs northwards along the western boundary of the airfield while the A167 running towards the village of Sandhutton marks its eastern extremity. Much of the land is used for turkey and pig farming. Parts of runway and perimeter track can still be seen and a few wartime buildings have survived for use by various industrial companies.

On the village green at Skipton-on-Swale is a memorial stone dedicated to the four Canadian squadrons that flew from the airfield. The cairn is in the shade of a Canadian maple tree and was erected to honour all those who served at the airfield during the Second World War, and the many civilians who supported them. The cairn marks the point where a crippled Halifax III of 433 Squadron came down on 5 August 1944 having returned from a bombing mission, killing two of the crew as well as a young boy, Kenneth Battensby, who was caught in the wreckage. The memorial was unveiled forty years later by Kenneth's brother and dedicated by a group including grateful survivors.

Summary of units based at Skipton-on-Swale during the Second World War

420 (Snowy Owl) Squadron RCAF (PT) – 6 Aug 42 (Waddington) – 14 Oct 42 (Middleton St George)
Wellington III

432 (Leaside) Squadron RCAF (QO) – 1 May 43 (Formed) – 17 Sep 43 (East Moor)
Wellington X

433 (Porcupine) Squadron RCAF (BM) – 25 Sep 43 (Formed) – 15 Oct 45 (Disbanded)
Halifax III (Nov 43 – Jan 45)
Lancaster I/III (Jan – Oct 45)

424 (Tiger) Squadron RCAF (QB) – 6 Nov 43 (North Africa) – 15 Oct 45 (Disbanded)
Halifax III (Nov 43 – Jan 45)
Lancaster I/III (Jan – Oct 45)

CHAPTER 27

Tholthorpe

Location – North Yorkshire, ten miles north-west of York.
Status – Satellite airfield. 62 (RCAF) Base – sub-station of Linton-on-Ouse.

Originally a grass airfield of the late 1930s, Tholthorpe opened in August 1940 and was allocated to 4 Group, Bomber Command, as a satellite for Linton-on-Ouse. The first visitors to the new site were Linton's Whitleys of 77

A Halifax of 434 Squadron RCAF. The Bluenoses formed at Tholthorpe in June 1943 but by the end of the year had left for their new home at Croft. (AHB)

Squadron and then Whitleys of 102 Squadron based at Topcliffe, but being all-grass Tholthorpe was never going to be able to sustain bomber operations during the winter months and so it closed again to undergo further construction work.

The airfield was eventually completed to the standard three-runway bomber design (the main runway being 2,000 yards long and aligned east–west, with two subsidiaries of 1,400 yards), but work had been slow and it was not until June 1943 that Tholthorpe re-opened. By then, the all-Canadian 6 (RCAF) Group had been formed and so Tholthorpe was allocated to the new group as a sub-station of 62 (RCAF) Base headquartered at Linton-on-Ouse.

Tholthorpe had been in existence for nearly three years without a resident squadron but things suddenly picked up when, in its opening month, a new Canadian squadron formed. This was 434 (Bluenose) Squadron RCAF and within days of the airfield re-opening the first Halifaxes started to arrive. Soon after came 431 (Iroquois) Squadron RCAF, a former Wellington squadron but now in the process of converting to the Halifax, which arrived from Burn during mid-July.

Tholthorpe had suddenly become one of Yorkshire's busiest airfields. 434 Squadron flew its first operations on the night of 12/13 August 1943 when ten of its aircraft made up part of a mixed Lancaster and Halifax force of more than 500 aircraft sent to bomb the Italian city of Milan. The raid was considered a success. 431 Squadron was operational soon after and both squadrons became fully involved in Bomber Command's major efforts. It was now the road to Berlin with raids against the Nazi capital starting to increase. However, with space becoming available at Croft, both squadrons left Tholthorpe for their new home, where they would remain for the rest of the war.

This time Tholthorpe would not be empty for long and just days later 425 (Alouette) Squadron RCAF arrived from Dishforth and 420 (Snowy Owl) Squadron RCAF from Dalton. Both squadrons had only recently returned from bases in North Africa and the Mediterranean where they had been operating Wellingtons in support of the Allied landings in Sicily and Italy. Having left their aircraft behind, the squadrons' personnel had returned to the UK by sea.

These two squadrons would remain at Tholthorpe for the rest of the war but it would take time for them to convert to the Halifax. By mid-February both were ready to resume operations and their first ops were flown on the night of 19/20 February 1944. Although it was still the height of the Battle of Berlin, the target on this occasion was Leipzig with an all-out effort of more than 800 aircraft taking part. But it was not a good night for Bomber Command and particularly for the Halifax force. Soon after crossing the Dutch coast the Main Force was intercepted by enemy night fighters and the bomber crews were continuously harassed all the way to the target. Furthermore, some of the crews arrived over the target to find it covered in cloud and that they were ahead of the Pathfinders, and so had to orbit before carrying out their attack. This was never a good situation to be in and seventy-eight bombers were lost that night, including thirty-four of the 255 Halifaxes involved in the raid (more than 13 per cent).

These latest losses led to the Halifax IIs and Vs being withdrawn from ops against targets in Germany, although the decision did not have any direct impact on Tholthorpe. Both its squadrons were equipped with the Halifax III and so the bombing offensive against Germany continued. But operating two heavy bomber squadrons from the airfield during the hard winter weather of early 1944 had caused problems. Even with its hardened runways and dispersals, it was not unusual for frozen or boggy conditions to prevent aircraft or vehicle movements, which led to a disruption in operations.

Tholthorpe was fortunate to escape relatively lightly from the horror of the Nuremberg raid at the end of March. With a total of ninety-five aircraft lost that night it turned out to be Bomber Command's worst night of the war but only one of Tholthorpe's twenty-six Halifaxes taking part in the raid was lost. That aircraft belonged to 425 Squadron and was flown by 23-year-old Flight Lieutenant John Taylor from Winnipeg. It was shot down by a night fighter. He and his crew are buried in the Durnbach War Cemetery in southern Germany.

Bomber Command now turned its attention to supporting the build up to Operation *Overlord* and both of Tholthorpe's Halifax squadrons were involved in attacks against enemy defences in northern France and disrupting enemy lines of communications.

Then, with the Allies having landed in Normandy, the squadrons supported the breakout towards Germany as well as taking part in attacks against the German V-weapon sites in northern France.

It was following one of these raids, against a V-1 flying-bomb site at Forêt d'Eawy on the night of 27/28 June 1944, that Tholthorpe witnessed an extraordinary act of courage by its 37-year-old base commander, Air Commodore Dwight Ross, who was visiting the airfield to speak to the returning crews about the raid. All of the Halifaxes had returned from the raid, but one aircraft belonging to 425 Squadron, flown by Sergeant M J P Lavoie, was making its approach on three engines.

On landing, Lavoie struggled to maintain control and veered off the runway into a parked Halifax, fully laden with fuel and bombs. Both aircraft immediately burst into flames with Lavoie's aircraft broken into three parts. Having seen what had happened, Ross immediately rushed to the scene and with the help of one of the ground crew, Corporal Maurice Marquet, pulled Lavoie from the wreckage.

Lavoie had suffered serious injuries but he was to be alright. However, ten 500 lb bombs in the second Halifax just yards away then exploded causing Ross and Marquet to be thrown

The site of the former bomber airfield is just to the north of Tholthorpe village. Overlooking what is now agricultural land is the original control tower, now a private residence. (Author)

to the ground in the blast. More cries could be heard from the rear turret of the crashed aircraft and despite the risk of further explosions, Ross and Marquet returned to the blazing wreckage in an attempt to release the gunner, Sergeant G C Rochon, who was trapped in his turret.

The port tail plane was burning furiously but Ross hacked away at the turret with an axe before handing it through the broken Perspex to Rochon. By now another member of the crew, Flight Sergeant Joseph St Germain, the bomb aimer, had arrived to assist and finally the rescuers were able to break through the turret's structure to free the rear gunner. But then another 500 lb bomb exploded, throwing the three rescuers to the ground in the blast. St Germain was the first to recover his senses and immediately threw himself across one of his colleagues to protect him from the flying debris.

Ross had suffered severe injuries during the rescue. His arm had been practically severed as a result of the second explosion but he was seen calmly walking to the ambulance; his arm was later amputated at the medical centre. Marquet, meanwhile, had spotted petrol running towards two aircraft nearby. With the help of two others, Melvin McKenzie and Robert Wolfe, both members of the crash tender who had also been caught up in the blast, the three airmen managed to move the aircraft from the vicinity and complete the rescue of the rear gunner.

For his leadership and courage in saving the lives of Lavoie and his rear gunner, Dwight Ross was awarded the George Cross while Joseph St Germain and Maurice Marquet each received the George Medal. Melvin McKenzie and Robert Wolfe, the two other airmen involved in the rescue, were both awarded the British Empire Medal.

These acts provide a fine example of the courage shown by members of the ground crew and station support personnel during the Second World War. Operating heavily armed bombers from an airfield was never without hazard. Furthermore, the war was far from over and Tholthorpe's worst night was yet to come when just weeks before the end of hostilities, nine of its Halifaxes failed to return from a raid on Chemnitz. It was the night of 5/6 March 1945 and the raid was a continuation of Operation *Thunderclap*, launched against the cities of Chemnitz,

Dresden and Leipzig, all identified as choke points standing in the way of the Russian advance on Berlin from the east.

While it was Dresden that made the headlines after the war, the raid against Chemnitz that night was also a massive one, with 760 aircraft taking part. But the night had got off to a bad start when nine aircraft from 6 (RCAF) Group crashed soon after take-off due to the icy conditions. Four of these were from Tholthorpe. Two were from 420 Squadron and these came down in the local area having appeared to stall due to a severe build-up of icing on the airframe and around the engines. One of the two aircraft lost from 425 Squadron appears to have crashed for a similar reason, while the other collided with another Halifax from Linton-on-Ouse; Linton also lost three aircraft due to icing.

Not only had most of the aircrew from Tholthorpe's four aircraft been killed, a number of civilians were also dead. And if that was not bad enough, three more of Tholthorpe's aircraft were lost over enemy territory during the raid, while another crashed on its way home and another force-landed elsewhere.

The last ops from Tholthorpe took place the following month with 420 Squadron's last raid being a daylight attack against Bremen on 22 April in preparation for an attack by the British XXX Corps, while 425's last op took place three days later against gun batteries on the Frisian island of Wangerooge.

With the war in Europe over, both Canadian squadrons were allocated to Tiger Force in preparation for a move to the Far East where the war against Japan was still raging. Both squadrons exchanged their Halifaxes for Canadian-built Lancaster Xs and returned to Canada to prepare for their move out to the Pacific. However, neither were to deploy as the Japanese surrender brought an end to the war in the Far East, and so both squadrons were disbanded.

With its aircraft gone, Tholthorpe closed to flying. As it was not to be part of the RAF's post-war plans, the airfield lay derelict for many years and was not disposed of until the 1950s, after which most of the land reverted to agriculture.

The site of this former wartime bomber airfield can be found just to the north of Tholthorpe village. Hag Lane, running northwards from the village, takes you along the western boundary of the airfield while the main East Coast railway line marks the eastern extremity. Parts of former runways and perimeter track can still

A granite memorial on the village green, with its inscription in English and French, stands as testament to the sacrifice made by the men of Tholthorpe's four Canadian squadrons during the Second World War. (Author)

be found. A few scattered buildings have survived, as has the former control tower, now a private residence. It can be seen by heading north from the village along the lane. After about 400 yards, and having passed the left turn into Derrings Lane, a track can be seen on your right with the control tower visible a hundred yards or so away. A granite memorial on the village green was erected by the people of Tholthorpe and surviving veterans. It stands as testament to the sacrifice made by the men of the four Canadian squadrons during the Second World War. Its inscription is in English and French and was unveiled in 1986 by Air Vice-Marshal Donald Bennett.

Summary of units based at Tholthorpe during the Second World War

434 (Bluenose) Squadron RCAF (WL) – 13 Jun 43 (Formed) – 10 Dec 43 (Croft)
Halifax V

431 (Iroquois) Squadron RCAF (SE) – 15 Jul 43 (Burn) – 9 Dec 43 (Croft)
Halifax V

425 (Alouette) Squadron RCAF (KW) – 12 Dec 43 (Dishforth) – 13 Jun 45 (Disbanded)
Halifax III (Dec 43 – May 45)
Lancaster X (May – Jun 45)

420 (Snowy Owl) Squadron RCAF (PT) – 12 Dec 43 (Dalton) – 12 Jun 45 (Disbanded)
Halifax III (Dec 43 – May 45)
Lancaster X (May – Jun 45)

CHAPTER 28

Topcliffe

Location – North Yorkshire, four miles south-west of Thirsk. Status – Operational and then a training airfield. HQ 61 (RCAF) Base.

On the edge of the Yorkshire Dales and close to the North Yorkshire Moors, Topcliffe led a rather unusual wartime existence. It started its life as an operational airfield under the control of 4 Group but ended the war as the centre of all training for 6 (RCAF) Group.

Built just to the north of the village from which the airfield takes its name, Topcliffe opened in September 1940 and was allocated to 4 Group, Bomber Command. It was then an all-grass airfield with brick-built maintenance hangars and buildings. The first aircraft to operate from the new airfield were Whitleys of 77 Squadron, under the command of a 34-year-old New Zealander, Wing Commander Geoffrey Jarman. The squadron had arrived from Linton-on-Ouse during October and the following month more Whitleys arrived at Topcliffe. These were from 102 Squadron, also from Linton.

Both squadrons were soon on operations but operating from an airfield so far north in England was not without its problems, particularly during the winter months when flying deep into Europe. Bad weather and a shortage of fuel often meant crews having to divert elsewhere. The problem had first become evident soon after arriving at Topcliffe. In those relatively early days of the bombing campaign there was little coordination between squadrons and no attempt to saturate targets with large numbers. And so the night of 23/24 November 1940 was typical of many at that stage of the war with Bomber Command sending its aircraft to a wide range of targets across France,

A Whitley of 77 Squadron, which was based at Topcliffe during the early part of the war. (RAF Leeming)

Germany and Italy. For the Topcliffe crews their target that night was a weapons factory in the Italian city of Turin but five aircraft, three from 102 and two from 77 Squadron, failed to return having become short of fuel. None of the three crews from 102 Squadron got further north than the south coast of England and were forced to ditch, bale out or force-land, while the two aircraft from 77 Squadron came down in East Anglia.

The two squadrons were to suffer further losses during their early months at Topcliffe and there can be no better example than the night of 27/28 June 1941. It was a night when Bomber Command sent more than a hundred aircraft to Bremen, a commercial and industrial city in north-west Germany with a large port on the River Weser, but seven aircraft failed to return to Topcliffe – four from 102 Squadron and three from 77.

The night was a disaster for two reasons. First, the crews reported intense night fighter activity during the raid; the first time such a report had been made. The second problem was the weather. Heavy storms and severe icing had caused the crews all sorts of problems. Of the thirty-five Whitleys taking part in the raid, eleven were lost, including the seven from Topcliffe.

Halifaxes of 102 Squadron preparing for another night raid during 1942. (AHB)

Three Wellingtons were also lost, bringing the total to fourteen (13 per cent of the force dispatched), which all added up to the Bremen raid being the worst night for Bomber Command to date. When looking at the Whitley losses alone, the loss rate was an alarming 31.4 per cent!

Topcliffe's personnel mourned the loss of so many men in one night, more than twenty of whom were dead, and amongst the many tragic tales that night is that of Bernard Harpur from Glemsford in Suffolk, the young sergeant pilot of a Whitley of 77 Squadron. Having run the gauntlet of flak over Bremen, during which his aircraft had been hit, and then having escaped the seemingly constant presence of enemy night fighters, Harpur had managed to get his aircraft back across the North Sea and heading for home. His Whitley was damaged and its engine leaking glycol but Harpur had nursed the aircraft to within sight of the Yorkshire coast but he was then forced to ditch the aircraft into the sea.

Ditching an aircraft of that size was never going to be easy. However, Harpur managed to get the Whitley down. His crew managed to abandon the sinking aircraft and get clear but they were to spend many hours in the sea before they were rescued two days later, owing their lives to their gallant young captain.

But Harpur had drifted away alone and had not survived the ordeal. His body was found close to where his crew had been picked up and was buried at his former home in Glemsford (St Mary) Churchyard. Bernard Harpur was just nineteen years old. He was the son of the Reverend Alexander Harpur of that same church. It is truly a sad tale.

Being an all-grass airfield and having initially been built with the most basic of infrastructure, Topcliffe lacked the hardened runways and facilities to accommodate the new heavy bombers entering service and so by late 1941 both squadrons had moved out. First to go was 77 Squadron, to Leeming in September, followed two months later by 102, which moved to the new airfield at Dalton.

Work began in the winter of 1941 to bring Topcliffe up to the standard required for a heavy bomber airfield. Three concrete runways were constructed, the main being 2,000 yards long and aligned north-east to south-west, with a perimeter track and hard standings for up to thirty-six aircraft, and enough accommodation for more than 2,000 personnel. By the following summer enough work had been complete to allow the first heavy bombers to move in. These were Halifax IIs belonging to 102 Squadron, which had re-equipped at Dalton and now returned to Topcliffe in June 1942 to complete its work-up with its new type.

The squadron flew its first operations with the Halifax in early August but its second spell at the airfield was only short-lived. Topcliffe was destined for the Canadians and so two months later 102 moved to Pocklington, from where the squadron would operate for the rest of the war, exchanging places with 405 (Vancouver) Squadron RCAF, which made the opposite journey the following day.

With the first Canadians having moved in, it was not long before a second Canadian squadron arrived. However, it was not to be more Halifaxes that arrived at Topcliffe but Wellingtons of 419 (Moose) Squadron RCAF under the command of 30-year-old Wing Commander Archie Walsh DFC AFC. However, the latest arrivals were not to remain at Topcliffe for long. Just a month later, 419 moved to Croft, its fourth home since the squadron had formed just nine months before, to convert to the Halifax but not before the loss of its CO. Walsh was killed on the night of 2/3 September during a raid on Karlsruhe; it was his twenty-ninth op.

With 419 Squadron gone, Topcliffe was again briefly home to two Canadian squadrons when 424 (Tiger) Squadron RCAF formed at Topcliffe in October 1942. But the arrival of its Wellingtons coincided with the departure of the Halifaxes, albeit temporarily, as 405 Squadron was transferred to Coastal Command to fly anti-submarine patrols from Beaulieu in the south of England.

As a Canadian base, Topcliffe was transferred to the newly formed 6 (RCAF) Group at the beginning of 1943. It was not long before 424 Squadron was ready to fly its first op and on the night of 15/16 January five of its Wellingtons joined sixty others to carry out an attack against the French Atlantic port of Lorient. The port was being used as a German U-boat base and the raid was the second on consecutive nights, with bombing on this second night reported to have been more accurate than the previous night with extensive damage to the port's buildings and surrounding area.

405 Squadron returned from its detachment to Coastal Command in early March but within days had moved on to Leeming. Topcliffe was now about to change role to one of training and so the following month 424 Squadron followed 405 out of the door.

Topcliffe now became the main training base for 6 (RCAF) Group. Designated Headquarters 61 (RCAF) Base, with its sub-stations at Dalton, Dishforth and Wombleton, the first Halifaxes of 1659 HCU had already arrived from Leeming and Topcliffe would be the HCU's home for the rest of the war. The airfield was also briefly home to Oxfords of 1535 BAT Flight during this period, although this unit disbanded during the summer.

As with all training bases there were several accidents involving crews from Topcliffe and many lives would be lost before the war was over. In November 1944 the airfield was transferred to 7 (Training) Group with Topcliffe re-designated 76 (RCAF) Training Base.

During the final months of the war the HCU exchanged its ageing Halifaxes for Canadian-built Lancaster Xs, but as the requirement to train more bomber crews reduced, Topcliffe's training task wound down. Then, with hostilities over the HCU

Topcliffe is now Alanbrooke Barracks, home to the 4th Regiment Royal Artillery, but RAF Topcliffe has survived as the airfield is still used as a relief landing ground for RAF Tucanos based at Linton-on-Ouse. (Author)

disbanded and Topcliffe was handed back to the RAF, after which the airfield was transferred to Transport Command.

Unlike many of Yorkshire's wartime bomber airfields, Topcliffe was to have a future in the post-war RAF. It was first a training airfield as home to the Air Navigation School, after which the airfield was transferred back to Transport Command. The merry-go-round continued when Topcliffe was transferred to Coastal Command, but by the end of the 1950s it had reverted to a training role once more. It now belongs to the army as Alanbooke Barracks, home to the 4th Regiment Royal Artillery, although RAF Topcliffe has survived as the airfield is still used as a relief landing ground for RAF Tucanos based at Linton-on-Ouse.

Alanbrooke Barracks is four miles south-west of Thirsk, to the north of the village of Topcliffe, between the A167 and A168. Understandably, access to the site is by prior permission only.

Summary of units based at Topcliffe during the Second World War

77 Squadron (KN) – 5 Oct 40 (Linton-on-Ouse) – 4 Sep 41 (Leeming)
Whitley V

102 Squadron (DY) – 15 Nov 40 (Linton-on-Ouse) – 14 Nov 41 (Dalton)
Whitley V

102 Squadron (DY) – 7 Jun 42 (Dalton) – 6 Aug 42 (Pocklington)
Halifax II

405 (Vancouver) Squadron (LQ) – 7 Aug 42 (Pocklington) – 13 Mar 43 (Leeming)
Halifax II
(Detached to Beaulieu from Oct 42 – Feb 43 on temporary transfer to Coastal Command)

419 (Moose) Squadron (VR) – 18 Aug 42 (Leeming) – 29 Sep 42 (Croft)
Wellington III

424 (Tiger) Squadron (QB) – 15 Oct 42 (Formed) – 18 Apr 43 (Leeming)
Wellington III

1659 HCU (FD) – 14 Mar 43 (Leeming) – 10 Sep 45 (Disbanded)
Halifax / Lancaster

Chapter 29

Wombleton (Welburn Hall)

Location – North Yorkshire, eight miles west of Pickering.
Status – Training airfield. 61 (RCAF) Base – sub-station of Topcliffe.

One of Yorkshire's last wartime airfields to be built was Wombleton. Constructed close to the North Yorkshire Moors, it was the highest of the county's airfields and because it was built close to the former First World War aerodrome at Welburn Hall, the new airfield was often referred to by the locals as its old name.

Wombleton opened in October 1943 and was allocated to the all-Canadian 6 (RCAF) Group as a sub-station of 61 (RCAF) Base headquartered by Topcliffe. Wombleton had been completed to the standard three-runway bomber design with concrete runways capable of supporting Bomber Command's heavy bombers. The main runway, nearly 2,000 yards long, was aligned east–west, while the two subsidiaries, each around 1,400 yards long, were orientated north-east to south-west and near north-south respectively; this latter runway utilized what was then the minor raid connecting the villages of Wombleton and Nunnington.

Being opened relatively late in the war, there was no immediate use for the new airfield as far as accommodating an operational squadron was concerned, and so with that in mind facilities at the airfield were only ever basic, to say the least. Furthermore, Wombleton's location meant that it suffered during periods of bad weather, and it was not unusual for the site to become a sea of mud. This led to obvious concerns about operating fully

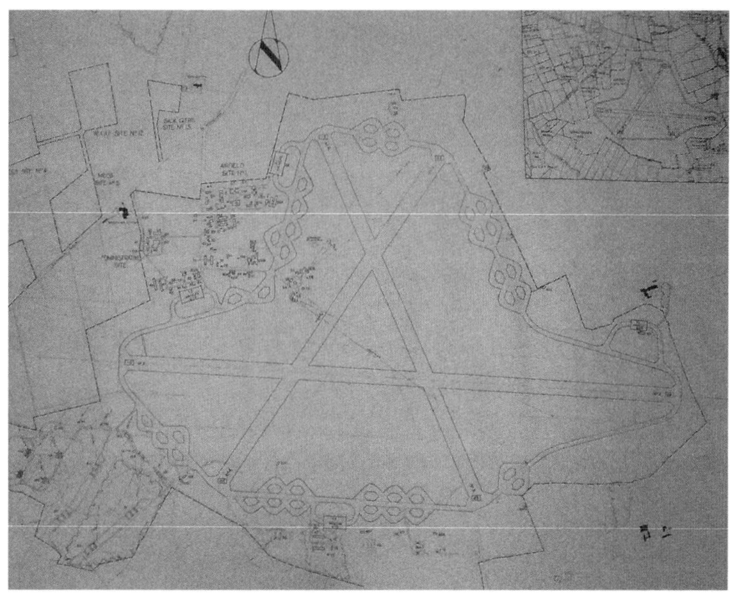

The layout of Wombleton, one of Yorkshire's last wartime airfields to have been built. (via Ken Delve)

laden heavy bombers from the airfield and so Wombleton's wartime role was to be a training one.

The first Halifaxes of 1666 HCU moved in from Dalton during October. The HCU would remain at Wombleton for the rest of the war and during early 1944 inherited a few Lancasters after 1679 HCU had briefly used the airfield before disbanding. Then, later in the year, 1666 HCU received a number of Canadian-built Lancaster Xs to replace its ageing aircraft.

As the war entered its final months the task of training new bomber crews reduced and like other training airfields Wombleton was transferred to 7 (Training) Group at the end of 1944. When hostilities came to an end the HCU disbanded and the airfield was placed on care and maintenance.

For the next couple of years the airfield was under the control of a maintenance unit but eventually, with no long-term use for the airfield, the land was sold off. A number of former wartime buildings lay derelict for many years and most of the land has long reverted to agriculture, but part of the site has been used

The former airfield of Wombleton can be found to the south of the village. Hungerhill Lane runs through what was the eastern part of the airfield. It formed part of the north–south subsidiary runway that utilized the lane connecting the villages of Wombleton and Nunnington. The remains of this runway can be seen on the right of the lane when heading south and this is the point where it met the main runway, which crossed Hungerhill Lane at this point. (Author)

over the years by light aircraft for private flying.

This former wartime bomber airfield can be found to the south of Wombleton village. Following Main Street, turn left into Hungerhill Lane and this takes you to the northern part of the airfield. The lane continues south along what was the airfield's eastern boundary and follows the

To the south of Wombleton village, where Common Lane meets Moorfields Lane (leading to a caravan park), is a memorial to the Canadians of 6 (RCAF) Group and to the men and women who served at Wombleton during the Second World War. (Author)

line of the subsidiary runway that ran north–south and utilized the lane connecting the villages of Wombleton and Nunnington. Remains of this runway can clearly be seen through the thin hedge and line of trees on the right of the lane when heading south. After following the line of this former runway for about 400 yards you will see a gap in the hedge and a turning to your left onto a track. This is private land but you will see the remains of what was the main runway that ran almost east-west and crossed Hungerhill Lane at this point.

Instead of turning off Main Street into Hungerhill Lane to look at the runways, you can also continue south from the village of Wombleton along Common Lane. Just a few hundred yards later there is a turning left into Moorfields Lane leading to Wombleton Caravan Park. At this junction there is a memorial comprising a rough stone obelisk. It was dedicated in 2001 to the Canadians of 6 (RCAF) Group and to the men and women who served at Wombleton during the Second World War. The caravan park marks the north-western part of the airfield where a hangar and a number of aircraft dispersals stood. Large sections of the former runways and perimeter track have survived.

Summary of units based at Wombleton during the Second World War

1666 HCU – Oct 43 – Aug 45
Halifax II/V & Lancaster I/X

1679 HCU – Dec 43 – Jan 44
Lancaster

Part III

Other Bomber Airfields of Yorkshire

Not all of Yorkshire's bomber airfields came under the control of either 4 Group or 6 (RCAF) Group. With county borders being the way they were, two of South Yorkshire's wartime bomber airfields – Finningley and Lindholme – were under the control of Bomber Command's 1 Group or 5 Group, which operated from airfields in neighbouring Lincolnshire. Both of these airfields are included here. Also included for completion are two other airfields used by Bomber Command. One was Doncaster, which spent most of the war under the control of Transport Command but was used at either end of hostilities by aircraft of Bomber Command. The other airfield, Yeadon, was a factory airfield for Avro. As a production site for the Lancaster it was a key part of Bomber Command's story in Yorkshire.

Chapter 30

Doncaster

Location – South Yorkshire, adjacent to Doncaster race course.
Status – 5 Group Bomber Command and then Transport Command.

Although the history of this site dates back more than a hundred years, when Doncaster race course was first used for an aviation meeting, and then as a landing ground during the First World War, Doncaster was not one of Bomber Command's operational airfields during the Second World War.

As an all-grass civil airfield between the wars it was only natural that Doncaster should be considered for further development but it seemingly lacked the facilities to become a main bomber airfield. It was, however, used during the very early days of the Second World War when Doncaster was home to the Avro Ansons and Handley Page Hampdens of 7 Squadron, a squadron then being used as a training unit for 5 Group, Bomber Command, although the squadron moved to Finningley just as hostilities were about to get underway.

Doncaster later became home to various transport and communications aircraft of 217 Squadron, a diverse unit providing assistance to all of the RAF's commands in areas such as the moving of squadron equipment and personnel between bases, and during 1941/42 the airfield was used by Lysanders and Tomahawks of 613 Squadron. Then, as a satellite of nearby Finningley during the latter period of the war, the Wellingtons of 18 OTU became frequent visitors to Doncaster as the demand for training more bomber crews increased. But when the OTU disbanded at the end of 1944 it brought an end to the visiting bombers, although the airfield was still used by various transport aircraft during the final months of the war.

Life at the airfield during the post-war period was quiet and as the town of Doncaster expanded the days of the old grass airfield were over. The former airfield has long disappeared, although the Doncaster race course on the junction of the A638 and A18 Leger Way, on the south-east part of the town, marks its approximate location.

Summary of units based at Doncaster during the Second World War

7 Squadron – 1 – 14 Sep 39
Anson I/Hampden I

CHAPTER 31

Finningley

Location – South Yorkshire, seven miles south-east of Doncaster.
Status – 5 Group and then a training airfield of Bomber Command.

Finningley is now the site of Robin Hood Airport and one of the RAF's most famous post-Second World War; it is an airfield with a long and cherished history dating back to the mid-1930s. As part of the RAF's Expansion Plan, farmland to the west of the village, by which the airfield takes its name, was identified as suitable for development as an airfield.

Built on flat plain land between two main roads, the A638 and A614, on the county borders of South Yorkshire, Lincolnshire and Nottinghamshire, Finningley officially opened in September 1936. It was then a grass airfield with five hangars and many technical and administrative buildings, under the command of a former First World War pilot, 42-year-old Wing Commander Arthur Gallehawk.

Initially allocated to 3 Group, Bomber Command, Finningley was a busy airfield during the build up to war, with many squadrons and aircraft types coming and going during the next three years. By the outbreak of the Second World War the airfield had been transferred to 5 Group with its two resident squadrons, 7 Squadron and 76 Squadron, equipped with Hampdens and Ansons. Both squadrons were then being used in the training role for the group's new bomber crews and were soon to move to Upper Heyford in Oxfordshire.

They were replaced by 106 Squadron, also equipped with Hampdens and Ansons, which continued where its predecessors had left off in the training role for the squadrons of 5 Group.

Between March and April 1940 the airfield was briefly home to Fairey Battles of 98 Squadron, which arrived from Scampton prior to crossing the Channel to France. This was just one of several comings and goings during what was later called the Phoney War. 7 Squadron came back and then went away again, and then when France fell the Battles of 12 Squadron arrived having returned from France before moving out again just two weeks later.

As the war reached a new phase, 106 Squadron ceased training and in early September 1940 flew its first minelaying operational sorties, a role it would specialize in during the following months. There were breaks in minelaying ops, though, as the squadron's crews joined those from other Hampden squadrons in carrying out attacks on German invasion barges waiting in the occupied ports across the Channel. In early 1941 the Hampdens were joined by Blenheims and Ansons of 7 Blind Approach Training Flight, later re-numbered 1507 BATF, before 106 Squadron moved to Coningsby in February, although some of its personnel remained behind to form the nucleus of 25 OTU.

Finningley's brief operational role was over as the station took up its new role of training. Now part of 7 (Operational Training) Group, Finningley would remain a training airfield for the rest of the war. However, although no longer operational, the airfield was still bombed twice in the following month. There were two further attacks during the next couple of months, although none of these seemed to have caused too much damage.

With Bomber Command expanding the training task increased out of all proportion. Because of the large number of student crews passing through the OTU, the airfield could not handle the increased amount of circuit work and airfield approaches required for pilot and crew training and so two nearby airfields at Bircotes and Bawtry, just across the county border, were used as satellites.

Over the next year the OTU's Hampdens were gradually phased out, as were the Manchesters that had briefly been part of the unit, and by May 1942 the OTU was equipped with Wellingtons. Administrative changes within Bomber Command meant that Finningley was now part of 92 Group and when every available bomber was required for the first Thousand

Bomber raid against Cologne at the end of the month thirty of the OTU's Wellingtons were involved. One aircraft failed to return, although the crew survived to be taken as prisoners of war. It had been the first of Harris' all-out efforts and when he repeated the Thousand Bomber idea just two nights later against Essen, and then again in June, this time against Bremen, the OTU was again involved.

With the Thousand Bomber raids over, the OTU resumed its training task but continued providing Wellingtons and instructor crews to supplement Bomber Command's Main Force whenever required. More minor tinkering within Bomber Command saw Finningley transferred to 93 Group in September but by the beginning of 1943 the huge training task over the past couple of years had put a strain on the airfield and its facilities. Finningley was now looking very tired and needed to be refurbished. However, the idea to construct hardened runways was put on hold and so the airfield would remain grass for the time being at least, although its main runway, running from the north-east of the airfield to the south-west, was extended to 2,000 yards.

By March 1943, work was complete and flying resumed, this time with 18 OTU as the airfield's main resident unit. It was manned with a mix of RAF and Polish personnel and had the task of feeding new bomber crews to squadrons of 1 Group based just across the county border in northern Lincolnshire. It was mostly equipped with Wellingtons, although the OTU also used other types for target towing. The airfield was also home to 1 Group's Communications Flight and to 1521 BATF, which had replaced 1507 in the spring of 1943.

With so many different units, each operating a variety of aircraft, Finningley was too crowded and so units started to move out. The airfield still needed a major upgrade and so flying ceased in November to allow the construction of three hardened runways and accommodation for up to 3,000 personnel. By May 1944, work was complete and so the Wellingtons of 18 OTU moved back in. However, by the end of the year there was no further need to train so many bomber crews and so the OTU disbanded. It was replaced by a new unit, the Bomber Command Instructor's School, which formed in early 1945. The school had a mix of aircraft – Lancasters, Halifaxes and Wellingtons – as well as some Spitfires and Hurricanes for fighter affiliation, with its

When the Second World War broke out, Finningley belonged to 5 Group, Bomber Command, but its brief operational existence came to an end in early 1941 when it became a training airfield, a role it maintained for the rest of the war. Retained in the post-war era, Finningley was one of the RAF's busiest airfields before it closed in the 1990s to be developed as what is now Robin Hood Airport Doncaster Sheffield. Shown here is a Dominie of 6 Flying Training School during the 1980s. (Author)

instructors including some of the command's most experienced aircrew to teach all kinds of tactics and procedures.

After the war Finningley was retained by the post-war RAF. Many training units came and went before it was decided that Finningley was to become a V-bomber base. The airfield was transferred back to Bomber Command and a new extended runway built, although the station's task of training did not disappear altogether as it was given the responsibility of training all Vulcan crews throughout the 1960s. By 1970 the airfield had been transferred to Training Command. Finningley then became one of the RAF's busiest stations until it was closed in 1996 to be developed as an international airport, opening in 2005 as Robin Hood Airport Doncaster Sheffield. The airport is seven miles to the south-east of Doncaster, on the eastern side of the A638 Great North Road and the western side of the A614 on the corner of Finningley village.

Summary of units based at Finningley during the Second World War

7 Squadron – 15 Sep 39 (Doncaster) – 23 Sep 39 (Upper Heyford)
Anson I/Hampden I

76 Squadron – Apr 37 (Formed) – 22 Sep 39 (Upper Heyford)
Anson I/Hampden I

106 Squadron – 6 Oct 39 (Cottesmore) – 22 Feb 41 (Coningsby)
Hampden I

98 Squadron – 19 Mar 40 (Scampton) – 15 Apr 40 (France)
Battle I

7 Squadron – 30 Apr 40 (Upper Heyford) – 20 May 40 (Leeming)
Hampden I

12 Squadron – 16 Jun 40 (France) – 2 Jul 40 (Binbrook)
Battle I

25 OTU – 1 Mar 41 – 1 Feb 43
Wellington/Anson

18 OTU – 25 Jan 43 – 30 Jan 45
Wellington/Anson

Chapter 32

Lindholme (Hatfield Woodhouse)

Location – South Yorkshire, seven miles north-east of Doncaster.
Status – Bomber Command airfield of 5 Group, then 1 Group, after which it became a training airfield.

Having been identified as suitable for the construction of an airfield as part of the RAF's Expansion Scheme, work began on Hatfield Moors to the east of Doncaster during the late 1930s. But work was still incomplete by the outbreak of the Second World War and so it was not until June 1940 that the airfield was opened as part of 5 Group, Bomber Command.

When it first opened the airfield was grass and called Hatfield Woodhouse, named after the nearby village, and was under the command of Group Captain E F Wareing DFC AFC. The first arrivals were Hampdens of 50 Squadron, which moved in from Waddington the following month under a new CO, Wing Commander G W Golledge, who had only just taken over command of the squadron following the death of its previous commanding officer. The squadron flew its first ops from Hatfield Woodhouse just two nights after its arrival. The target was Hamburg but the weather was so bad that only two of the eleven aircraft sent on the raid made it back, the others having to put down elsewhere.

The airfield was re-named Lindholme in August 1940 to avoid confusion with Hatfield in Hertfordshire. For the rest of the year the squadron was involved in a variety of operations, including minelaying, attacks on invasion barges gathered in the occupied

Following a similar path to its neighbouring Finningley, Lindholme spent the early days of the Second World War as an operational airfield of 5 Group. It then transferred to Bomber Command's 1 Group and became home to two Polish Wellington squadrons until late 1942 when it became a training airfield. After the war Lindholme was used for many years as a relief landing ground for Finningley before closing in the 1980s, after which part of the site was developed as HMP Lindholme. (via Ken Delve)

ports just across the Channel, attacks on German naval shipping as well as attacks against other industrial targets in Germany and even Berlin.

At the end of the year Golledge handed over command of 50 Squadron to Gus Walker, a pre-war pilot from Leeds who had played rugby for Yorkshire and England. Walker would guide the squadron through what turned out to be a difficult year, earning the DSO and DFC, before working his way up the ranks within Bomber Command as a station commander (Syerston) and a base commander (42 Base at Pocklington) before finishing the war as 4 Group's Senior Air Staff Officer.

In June 1941, Lindholme was briefly home to a second Hampden squadron. This was 408 (Goose) Squadron RCAF, which formed under the command of Wing Commander Nelles Timmerman, a 28-year-old from Kingston, Ontario. It was the

RCAF's second squadron to form overseas but after taking delivery of its first aircraft the following month the Canadians moved to Syerston – the same day that 50 Squadron moved to Swinderby.

Lindholme was then transferred to 1 Group as two Polish Wellington squadrons made the opposite journey from Syerston. These were 304 'Slaski' Squadron and 305 'Weilkopolski' Squadron, both of which commenced operations soon after they arrived. For the next ten months the two Polish squadrons operated side-by-side from Lindholme, taking part in most of Bomber Command's major efforts, before, in May 1942, 304 was transferred to Coastal Command.

305 Squadron was now Lindholme's only resident unit and later that month thirteen of its crews took part in the first Thousand Bomber raid against Cologne, and then the follow up mass efforts against Essen and Bremen. During the last of these the squadron lost its commanding officer, 43-year-old Lieutenant-Colonel Stanislaw Skarzynski. It was a huge blow, not only for the squadron but also for Poland. Skarzynski had become a public figure following his transatlantic solo flight before the war and had been serving in an attaché role in Romania when the Second World War broke out. From there he had managed to help a number of Polish pilots flee their homeland and make their way across Europe to England. Then, having made his own way to England he had been given command of Polish flying schools in England. However, Skarzynski had not wanted to spend the war on the side lines and had requested a combat posting, leading to his appointment in command of 305 Squadron at Lindholme. While returning from Bremen across the North Sea in his heavily damaged Wellington, and with one engine out, he was forced to ditch in bad weather. His crew managed to get out and survived but Skarzynski was the last to leave the sinking aircraft and was washed out to sea.

A month later the squadron moved to Hemswell in Lincolnshire so that Lindholme could undergo major redevelopment. Rather unusually, two hardened runways, crossing at ninety degrees, were constructed rather than the normal three for a bomber airfield. The main, 2,000 yards long, ran from the north-east to south-west while the second, 1,400 yards in length, was aligned south-east to north-west. They were connected by a hardened perimeter track with thirty-six hard standings for the dispersal of aircraft, with five hangars for maintenance and enough accommodation for 2,500 personnel.

The new airfield was ready for the arrival of four-engine heavy bombers but Lindholme was no longer to be an operational airfield and would spend the rest of the war in the training role. By October 1942, enough work was complete to allow the Lancasters and Manchesters of 1656 HCU to move in from Breighton with the task of training 1 Group's new bomber crews for the Lancaster.

Lindholme was now a major training airfield for 1 Group and home to a variety of other aircraft – Whitleys, Wellingtons, Defiants, Lysanders and Martinets – including aircraft of 1481 Target Towing Flight tasked with the training of the group's navigators and air gunners. At the beginning of 1943, Oxfords of 1503 Blind Approach Training Flight also arrived. This was another of 1 Group's training units and tasked with teaching pilots blind landing techniques, particularly important during the winter months when crews would return to their airfields in all kinds of weather. Then, in June, 1667 HCU formed as the group's second HCU at Lindholme with Lancasters and Halifaxes.

Under the RAF's re-organization of airfields, Lindholme became Headquarters 11 Base, with Faldingworth and Blyton, both in Lincolnshire, as its sub-stations. The merry-go-round of training units continued throughout the following months. 1503 BATF disbanded and then 1667 HCU moved to Faldingworth to free up space at Lindholme for the formation of 1 Lancaster Finishing School. The school ran three flights with its headquarters and one flight at Lindholme, and the other flights at Blyton and Faldingworth. However, further tinkering with 1 Group's training units and their airfields led to the HQ element leaving Lindholme in early 1944 for Hemswell, with its flight following in the spring.

With the war entering its final phase, Lindholme's training task gradually reduced and by the end of hostilities the airfield had been transferred to 7 (Training) Group. 1656 HCU was then disbanded, although Lindholme was retained by the post-war RAF until the 1980s. Part of the former airfield is now HMP Lindholme, a Category C prison, and can be found seven miles north-east of Doncaster on the A614 Bawtry Road, to the south of the village of Hatfield Woodhouse. As you travel northwards along the A614, past the prison entrance on your right, the land that was once the airfield is on your right.

Summary of units based at Lindholme during the Second World War

50 Squadron (VN) – 10 Jul 40 (Waddington) – 18 Jul 41 (Swinderby)
Hampden I

408 (Goose) Squadron RCAF (EQ) – 24 Jun 41 (Formed) – 18 Jul 41 (Syerston)
Hampden I

304 'Slaski' Squadron – 19 Jul 41 (Syerston) – 9 May 42 (Tiree)
Wellington I

305 'Weilkopolski' Squadron – 20 Jul 41 (Syerston) – 22 Jul 42 (Hemswell)
Wellington II

1656 HCU – 1 Oct 42 – 10 Nov 45
Manchester / Lancaster / Halifax

1667 HCU – 1 Jun 43 – 8 Oct 43
Lancaster / Halifax

CHAPTER 33

Yeadon

Location – West Yorkshire, six miles north-west of Leeds.
Status – Factory Airfield (Avro) used by Bomber Command.

Now the site of Leeds Bradford airport, the history of Yeadon dates back to before the Second World War when it was developed on Yeadon Moor as an all-grass municipal aerodrome. The RAF established a presence during the mid-1930s with the formation of an auxiliary air squadron, 609 (West Riding) Squadron, as a day bomber squadron of the Royal Auxiliary Air Force.

It is not surprising that the site was considered for further military development and during the years leading up to the Second World War the airfield was home to Hawker Hart light-bombers. These were later replaced by Hawker Hinds, by which time a temporary hangar had been built on the north-west corner of the airfield to accommodate the aircraft.

By the outbreak of war, 609 had become a fighter squadron, with its Spitfires moving to Catterick. With all civil flying at Yeadon suspended, the airfield was requisitioned by the RAF and allocated to Fighter Command. However, the airfield was too far north to be of much use to RAF fighters during the first year of war and so Yeadon was increasingly used by Bomber Command as one of its scatter airfields for its Yorkshire-based squadrons, particularly those of 4 Group based at Linton-on-Ouse, as well as by the group's maintenance organization and communications flight.

In early 1941 Yeadon was transferred to Flying Training Command and then a year later the airfield was taken over by the Ministry of Aircraft Production for its nearby Avro factory. Given the increase in aircraft production in Yorkshire, particularly with Yeadon having become the main site for the production of the Anson (over 4,500 were built at the factory) and one of the main sites for Lancaster production (nearly 700 were eventually built at the factory), significant improvements were made to the airfield, including the lengthening of its runway. Yeadon quickly became a key site for aircraft production and testing. It had also been necessary to build new technical, administrative and domestic buildings, as well as accommodation and social facilities for the factory's huge workforce, which at its peak during 1944 exceeded well over 10,000 people.

After the war aircraft production at Yeadon ceased. With there being no military requirement to retain the site, civilian flights recommenced and 609 Squadron moved back in. The RAF retained a presence until the late-1950s, after which the airfield gradually grew in size to become Leeds Bradford Airport. It is seven miles to the north-west of Leeds city centre, to the north-east of Yeadon on the A658.

Appendix 1

Bomber Command Order of Battle (Operational Squadrons Based in Yorkshire Only)– 1 September 1939

4 Group		
10 Sqn	Dishforth	Whitley IV
51 Sqn	Linton-on-Ouse	Whitley II/III
58 Sqn	Linton-on-Ouse	Whitley III
77 Sqn	Driffield	Whitley III/V
78 Sqn	Dishforth	Whitley I/IV/V
97 Sqn	Leconfield	Whitley II/III
102 Sqn	Driffield	Whitley III
166 Sqn	Leconfield	Whitley I
5 Group		
7 Sqn	Finningley	Hampden I and Anson I
76 Sqn	Finningley	Hampden I and Anson I

Appendix 2

Bomber Command Order of Battle (Operational Squadrons Based in Yorkshire and County Durham only) – January 1944 (Battle of Berlin)

4 Group

10 Sqn	Melbourne	Halifax II
51 Sqn	Snaith	Halifax II/III
76 Sqn	Holme-on-Spalding Moor	Halifax V
77 Sqn	Elvington	Halifax II
78 Sqn	Breighton	Halifax II/III
102 Sqn	Pocklington	Halifax II
158 Sqn	Lissett	Halifax II/III
466 Sqn (RAAF)	Leconfield	Halifax III
578 Sqn	Snaith	Halifax III
640 Sqn	Leconfield	Halifax III

6 (RCAF) Group

408 Sqn RCAF	Linton-on-Ouse	Lancaster II
419 Sqn RCAF	Middleton St George	Halifax II
420 Sqn RCAF	Tholthorpe	Halifax III
424 Sqn RCAF	Skipton-on-Swale	Halifax III
425 Sqn RCAF	Tholthorpe	Halifax III
426 Sqn RCAF	Linton-on-Ouse	Lancaster II

427 Sqn RCAF	Leeming	Halifax V/III
428 Sqn RCAF	Middleton St George	Halifax V/III
429 Sqn RCAF	Leeming	Halifax II/V
431 Sqn RCAF	Croft	Halifax V
432 Sqn RCAF	East Moor	Lancaster II
433 Sqn RCAF	Skipton-on-Swale	Halifax III
434 Sqn RCAF	Croft	Halifax V

APPENDIX 3

Bomber Command Order of Battle (Operational Squadrons Based in Yorkshire and County Durham Only) – January 1945

4 Group		
10 Sqn	Melbourne	Halifax III
51 Sqn	Snaith	Halifax III
76 Sqn	Holme-on-Spalding Moor	Halifax III
77 Sqn	Full Sutton	Halifax III
78 Sqn	Breighton	Halifax III
102 Sqn	Pocklington	Halifax III
158 Sqn	Lissett	Halifax III
346 (French) Sqn	Elvington	Halifax III
347 (French) Sqn	Elvington	Halifax III
466 Sqn (RAAF)	Driffield	Halifax III
578 Sqn	Burn	Halifax III
640 Sqn	Leconfield	Halifax III
6 (RCAF) Group		
408 Sqn RCAF	Linton-on-Ouse	Halifax III
415 Sqn RCAF	East Moor	Halifax III
419 Sqn RCAF	Middleton St George	Lancaster X

420 Sqn RCAF	Tholthorpe	Halifax III
424 Sqn RCAF	Skipton-on-Swale	Lancaster I/III
425 Sqn RCAF	Tholthorpe	Halifax III
426 Sqn RCAF	Linton-on-Ouse	Halifax VII
427 Sqn RCAF	Leeming	Halifax III
428 Sqn RCAF	Middleton St George	Lancaster X
429 Sqn RCAF	Leeming	Halifax III
431 Sqn RCAF	Croft	Lancaster X
432 Sqn RCAF	East Moor	Halifax VII
433 Sqn RCAF	Skipton-on-Swale	Lancaster I/III
434 Sqn RCAF	Croft	Lancaster X

Bibliography

Bennett, Air Vice-Marshal D C T, *Pathfinder* (Sphere Books Ltd, London, 1958).

Bishop, Patrick, *Bomber Boys: Fighting Back 1940–45* (Harper Press, London, 2007).

Bowyer, Chaz, *For Valour: The Air V.C.s* (William Kimber & Co Ltd, London, 1978).

Charlwood, Don, *No Moon Tonight* (first published by Angus & Robertson, Australia, 1956).

Delve, Ken, *The Source Book of the RAF* (Airlife Publishing Ltd, Shrewsbury, 1994).

Delve, Ken, *The Military Airfields of Britain: Northern England* (The Crowood Press Ltd, Marlborough, 2006).

Delve, Ken and Jacobs, Peter, *The Six-Year Offensive* (Arms and Armour Press, London, 1992).

Franks, Norman, *Claims to Fame: The Lancaster* (Arms and Armour Press, London, 1994).

Halfpenny, Bruce Barrymore, *Action Stations 4: Military Airfields of Yorkshire* (Patrick Stephens Ltd, Cambridge, 1982).

Halley, James J, *The Squadrons of the Royal Air Force and Commonwealth 1918–1988* (Air-Britain (Historians) Ltd, Tonbridge, 1988).

Jacobs, Peter, *The Lancaster Story* (Arms and Armour Press, London, 1996).

Jacobs, Peter, *Bomb Aimer Over Berlin: The Wartime Memoires of Les Bartlett DFM* (Pen & Sword Books Ltd, Barnsley, 2007).

Jacobs, Peter, *Bomber Command Airfields of Lincolnshire* (Pen & Sword Aviation, Barnsley, 2016).

Mennell, Brian, *Wings Over York: The History of Rufforth Airfield* (Fox 3 Publishing, York, 2012).

Mennell, Gary, and Mennell, Brian, *Slightly Below the Glide Path IV: RAF Linton-on-Ouse* (Fox Publishing, York, 2015).

Middlebrook, Martin, *The Battle of Hamburg: The Firestorm Raid* (Cassell & Co, London, 1980).

Middlebrook, Martin, *The Berlin Raids* (Viking, the Penguin Group, London, 1988).

Middlebrook, Martin, and Everitt, Chris, *The Bomber Command War Diaries: An Operational Reference Book 1939–1945* (Penguin Books, London, 1990).

Musgrove, Gordon, *Pathfinder Force: A History of 8 Group* (first published by Macdonald & Jane's, London, 1976).

Otter, Patrick, *Yorkshire Airfields in the Second World War* (Countryside Books, Newbury, 1998).

Rapier, Brian J, *Halifax at War* (Ian Allan, London, 1987).

Rolfe, Mel, *Looking into Hell: Experiences of the Bomber Command War* (Arms and Armour Press, London, 1995).

Searby, John, *The Bomber Battle for Berlin* (Guild Publishing, London, 1991).

Sweetman, John, *Bomber Crew: Taking on the Reich* (Abacus, London, 2004).